JUDAISM FOR TODAY

JUDAISM FOR TODAY

JOHN D. RAYNER AND BERNARD HOOKER

UNION OF LIBERAL AND
PROGRESSIVE SYNAGOGUES

THE AUTHORS

RABBI JOHN D. RAYNER, M.A., has been Senior Minister of the Liberal Jewish Synagogue, St. John's Wood, London, since 1961 and also teaches rabbinic students at the Leo Baeck College. He has co-edited the prayerbooks of the Union of Liberal and Progressive Synagogues and his publications include *Towards Mutual Understanding between Jews and Christians* and *Guide to Jewish Marriage*.

.Born in Germany in 1924, he came to England as a child refugee in 1939, continued his education at Durham School and, after four years' Army service as an infantry officer, went to Emmanuel College, Cambridge, on a scholarship. There he spent six years, reading Modern Languages, then Moral Science, then Hebrew, and gained First Class honours. Later he was for two years a postgraduate student at the Hebrew Union College, Cincinnati, Ohio, U.S.A.

He has been Minister of the South London Liberal Synagogue, Chairman of the European Board of the World Union for Progressive Judaism and Chairman of the Council of Reform and Liberal Rabbis in Britain.

RABBI BERNARD HOOKER, B.A., H.C.F., was born in London. He received his theological training at Jews' College and obtained a B.A. honours degree at London University. He was the youngest Chaplain to be appointed to the Armed Forces, in which capacity he served as Jewish Chaplain to 1 Corps, British Army on the Rhine, and later as Senior Jewish Chaplain to the Middle East Land Forces.

After demobilization, he served as Minister to the Birmingham Progressive Synagogue and the Wembley Liberal Synagogue until he was invited in 1965 to become the Spiritual Leader of the Jewish Community in Jamaica. While in the West Indies, he produced a number of books, including *The Rabbi Speaks*, *The Bible, Judaism and Jamaica* and *Prophets and Seers*. He was also appointed a Director of the Jamaica Broadcasting Corporation, in recognition of his outstanding contribution to radio and television in that island.

In 1975, he returned to the United Kingdom to become Minister of the North London Progressive Synagogue. He has been a Vice-President of the Union of Liberal and Progressive Synagogues for many years.

Printed and bound by Hazell Watson & Viney Ltd.,
Aylesbury, Bucks.

Contents

Foreword

I THE THEORY OF LIBERAL JUDAISM

Chapter   *Page*

1 How Beautiful our Heritage
  Liberal Judaism affirms Judaism   3

2 The Heritage of the Congregation of Jacob
  The religious character of Judaism   6

3 Sing to the Lord a New Song
  The need for reform   9

4 The Seal of God
  The need for intellectual integrity   13

5 The Beginning of Wisdom
  The existence of God   18

6 Our God and our Fathers' God
  The Jewish conception of God   22

7 A Little Less Than Divine
  The Jewish conception of man   28

8 The End of Days
The hope for a Messianic Age 34

9 A Light to the Nations
The mission of the Jewish people 39

10 The Word of the Lord
The progressive nature of Revelation 45

11 What does the Lord your God require of you?
The sovereignty of God's will 52

12 These are the things which you shall do
The priority of right conduct 59

13 That you may Remember
The value of observances 67

II THE PRACTICE OF LIBERAL JUDAISM

1 To Life!
The sanctity of life 75

2 Love your Neighbour
The Golden Rule 79

3 A Little Sanctuary
The sanctity of family life 83

4 Justice, Justice
The duty to promote social justice 88

Chapter		Page
5	Seek Peace and Pursue it *The duty to promote international peace*	94
6	You shall not Destroy *The duty to protect the environment*	99
7	To Learn and to Teach *The need for religious education*	106
8	The Service of the Heart *The importance of prayer*	111
9	The House of the Lord *The role of the Synagogue*	116
10	Observe the Sabbath Day *The value of the Sabbath*	123
11	Days of Awe *The High Holydays*	128
12	Three Times in the Year *The Pilgrimage Festivals*	133
13	Joy and Gladness *The minor feasts and fasts*	140
14	All your Children shall be Taught of the Lord *Rituals relating to birth and adolescence*	145
15	The Voice of the Bridegroom and the Voice of the Bride *Rituals relating to marriage*	151

16 Your God shall be my God
The acceptance of sincere proselytes 158

17 And a Time to Die
Rituals relating to death 163

REFERENCES 167

Illustrations

Plate 1. *The Sefer Torah*, the Scroll of the Law, opened to the beginning of the book of Leviticus together with the *Yad*, the pointer, and the pair of crowns. See p. 117.

Plate 2. The two Sabbath candles, the Kiddush wine and a Challah, a Sabbath loaf to initiate the home celebration of the Sabbath. See p. 124.

Plate 3. The special candle, the spice box, wine and the Liberal Jewish prayerbook, Service of the Heart, opened to the *Havdalah* service which concludes the Sabbath. See p. 126.

Plate 4. The Four Species used during the recitation of the Psalms of praise during the Festival of Sukkot. The palm, willow and myrtle branches and the citron. See p. 139.

Photographs by Frank Hellner.

Foreword

It is often supposed by non-Jews that, as the New follows the Old Testament and as Judaism preceded Christianity, the Jewish religion rightfully belongs to the past—and it is due only to the Jews' obstinacy or loyalty (depending on one's disposition towards Jews) that it has persisted into modern times.

Believing and practising Jews would affirm that this is not the case at all. Judaism has survived because it gave to its adherents a philosophy of God and the universe and a way of life which appealed so much to their reason and emotions that they were prepared to sacrifice their lives rather than give it up. One may love an antique possession, but one does not give one's life for it. Just so, the Judaism for which Jews have died was not an antiquated tradition, but a living faith.

According to the book of Deuteronomy, Moses said to the people of Israel as they were about to enter the Promised Land and after he had enumerated the laws by which they were to live: 'Choose life and live'. It has been the belief of Jews over millennia that only obedience to God's laws makes life livable and that non-obedience would spell their spiritual and physical destruction.

A living faith must change and grow. Judaism has done both. Even from the standpoint of the fundamentalist Jew who believes that every word of the Torah—the Five Books of Moses—came directly from God through Moses, the Judaism contained in those holy books is not the Judaism of the modern day. For example, where is the Temple? Where are the animal sacrifices? Where are the officiating priests? They have ceased to exist in Jewish life, not only because the Temple was destroyed by the Romans, but because they no longer reflect the spiritual growth in Judaism towards the democracy of the synagogue, the equality of prayer and the learning of the rabbis. It is significant that the Temple service, as portrayed in the Bible, has far more similarities to Catholic Christian worship than to the Jewish liturgy. One might argue that the Orthodox Jew prays for the restoration of the old ways, but many would maintain—and not un-fairly, in my view—that there is not even among the traditionalists the will to bring back the past. There is not a Jew, to my knowledge, who has ever seriously suggested that now the Old City of Jerusalem is in Jewish hands, the Temple should be rebuilt and Jewish priestcraft given a new lease of life.

If Judaism has changed over the centuries, despite the belief of the fundamentalists that its holiness rested in its spiritual proximity to the Revelation at Sinai, in the last century Judaism has changed through the initiative of Jewish scholars who attracted a large following to their radical belief that God's Revelation is continuous and does not end at one point in human history. As God spoke to Abraham, so he spoke to Moses—and as he spoke to Moses, so he spoke to Rabbi Akiva and so he speaks to the spiritual geniuses of every age.

The Talmud, the record of legal discussions and decisions, records that Moses was allowed to return to earth to visit the Law academy of Rabbi Akiva. There, he listened to the interpretations of the Mosaic Code, but could not understand the complexity of the legal arguments and was amazed, though reassured, when Akiva informed his disciples that this was the law as it was given to Moses at Sinai.

To keep the law alive and dynamic, in addition to the Torah, Judaism had an Oral Law, which, according to tradition, was also given to Moses, but which had to be passed down over the generations by word of mouth. It was forbidden to write down this Oral Law and thus the possibility of change and the ability of the leaders of each generation to make their contribution to their people's spiritual and social development was assured.

Unfortunately, difficult and unstable periods, several times in Jewish history, made the rabbis fear that unless the Oral Law was written down, it would be lost. Nevertheless, new oral traditions constantly developed. All this came to an end during the Middle Ages, when debates were no longer simply recorded, but, instead, rabbis of recognised brilliance and authority codified the Oral Law and put a final seal on what was to be done and what was not to be done.

The various codifications of the Oral Law led to a limitation of Jewish creativity, though there have been exceptional rabbis of genius who were able to find ambiguities even in the Codes, which allowed them to exercise creative ability. But, for the most part, Jewish life had become circumscribed by a mass of ritual law. It is the mark of the Jewish love of law and tradition, that, even within the restricted framework in which Jews lived, bound by the law from within and limited by a hostile Christian world from without, they were able to find much joy in living as Jews. Obviously, a way of life which had developed over 3,000 years had strained out most of the sand and had left spiritual gold.

Still, with the scientific and social enlightenment in Europe and the removal of civil restrictions on Jews, there had to arise Jewish scholars who would desire to reconcile Judaism with the fresh winds of modern thinking, just as Philo and Maimonides, each in their own age, felt compelled to reconcile Judaism with Platonism and Aristotelianism. These modern Jewish leaders took, as their departing point from tradition, the acceptance of modern biblical criticism, which stated that even the Mosaic Law developed over a long period, well after the death of Moses, but was attributed to him to give it the authority it required.

It should be mentioned here that there was nothing dishonest in this approach. In ancient days, everyone accepted the attribution of great works and laws to legendary heroes as a legitimate legal and literary device.

With this new approach to the Bible and Revelation, the reform of Judaism began in the 19th century in Germany and spread to the United States, where it developed strong roots. And with the new-found freedom which their belief in Progressive Revelation allowed them, the pioneers of Progressive Judaism made numerous changes in Jewish modes of worship and religious observance.

As a result of the tension which existed between Jewish and non-Jewish life, these innovators felt a double responsibility— to preserve the best in their tradition and to create new expressions of their religion, which would encourage the continued attachment of the modern Jew to his faith. The renewal of Judaism was particularly important, because the new discoveries of science, which had drawn so many Christians away from the Church, had no less an effect upon those Jews who, hungry to taste the scientific and artistic pleasures of the Western World from which they had been cut off for so many years, were prepared to cast off the religion of their fathers to enter a new, free world.

Seventy-five years ago, in 1902, a bold step was taken to renew Judaism in Britain by the formation of the Jewish Religion Union, led by Lily Montagu, Claude Montefiore and Israel Abrahams and supported by the Rev. Simeon Singer, Sir Isodore Spielman and other leaders of Anglo-Jewry. The Union began by organizing religious services designed to arrest the drift away from Judaism. Six years later, the words 'for the advancement of Liberal Judaism' were significantly added to the title: Jewish Religious Union.

In 1912, the Liberal Jewish Synagogue was established by the Jewish Religious Union and Israel Mattuck, European-born but American-trained, was appointed its first rabbi. Rabbi Dr. Mattuck gave profound spiritual leadership to the Movement which, since its inception, has founded 23 con-gregations, which are now known collectively as the UNION OF LIBERAL AND PROGRESSIVE SYNAGOGUES.

In *Judaism for Today—an ancient faith with a modern message*, Rabbi John D. Rayner, Senior Minister of the Liberal Jewish Synagogue, writes about the principles upon which Liberal Judaism was founded and the changes in Liberal Jewish theory over the last 75 years. Rabbi Bernard Hooker, Senior Minister of the North London Progressive Synagogue, deals with the practices of Liberal Judaism.

In the following pages, two leaders of our Movement restate clearly and succinctly the essence of Jewish belief and practice according to the Liberal and Progressive interpretation. In doing so, they are still affirming the Judaism which was begun by Abraham when he had both the Revelation of the One God who created the world and the vision of all men and women uniting to worship and obey their Creator.

This book was written in the hope that, by its restatement of Judaism, all Jews who read it will receive a clearer understanding of their faith and the practices of Judaism. For those who are not Jewish, the intention is that this book will enable them to realise the power that Judaism has wielded to keep the loyalty of its adherents since the beginning of Western history. That power derives from its life idealism, its belief that only through the practice of love, justice and kindness, as laid down by the Jewish tradition, can mankind reach that day for which Jews pray daily and which they hope to help make a reality: **On that day the Lord will be One and his name One.**

It is the everlasting belief in the possible realisation of the Messianic dream which entitles us to say of Judaism that it is today an ancient faith with a message which can never die.

(Rabbi) SIDNEY BRICHTO
Director and Executive Vice-President
UNION OF LIBERAL AND PROGRESSIVE SYNAGOGUES
London 1978

PART I

THE THEORY OF
LIBERAL JUDAISM

1 How Beautiful our Heritage

Liberal Judaism affirms Judaism

What is Liberal Judaism? That is not an easy question to answer. For Liberal Judaism has no official creed. It is true that in 1909 the Jewish Religious Union issued a pamphlet setting out the general principles which, it was thought, would commend themselves to its membership and that in the same year it adopted a manifesto outlining its practical programme. It is also true that from time to time individuals have attempted to state and re-state the Movement's standpoint. But none of these documents were ever intended to have any kind of binding authority. They were offered merely as guidelines which individuals were free to accept, modify or reject. Their purpose was to suggest, perhaps to persuade, never to dictate. Indeed, Judaism generally has never promulgated a creed binding on all Jews; and the emphasis on freedom implicit in Liberal Judaism's liberalism would make the imposition of such a creed doubly unacceptable to its adherents; it would be both un-Jewish and un-Liberal.

That being so, one might be inclined to say: Liberal Judaism is whatever any individual Liberal Jew takes it to be. But that would not only be unhelpful; it would also be, in an important sense, untrue. For the Movement does have a more or less coherent outlook, a more or less distinctive ethos, a more or less discernible thrust, pioneered by its founders, developed by their successors, reflected in its policies, expounded in its literature, distilled in its liturgy; and these unifying characteristics are not necessarily im-

3

mediately perceived or well understood by every novice who chooses to join a Liberal synagogue.

Therefore, while no single definition of Liberal Judaism can hope to satisfy every individual, nevertheless, if its true spirit is to be conveyed, a happy mean must be sought between the two extremes of defining it too rigidly or too loosely; and this requires an attempt to articulate the consensus of those best qualified to understand it, especially its rabbinic and non-rabbinic leaders. Accordingly, it is for them that we shall try to speak, and it is in this sense that we shall henceforth use, with due diffidence, the first person plural.

What then do 'we' affirm? First and foremost, we affirm Judaism. To promote the cause of Judaism—to defend and enhance its good name, to purify it, to strengthen it, to preserve it, to make it a vital force and an effective influence, and to transmit it successfully to the generations of the future—that is for us the whole purpose of the exercise. Therefore the noun in 'Liberal Judaism' is more important to us than the adjective. Nevertheless the adjective is important too, and for the same reason; for it points to the particular expression of Judaism which, as we believe, has the best chance of commending itself to modern Jews and therefore of ensuring the survival of Judaism as a whole. The noun defines the end, the adjective the means. We are Liberals for the sake of Judaism.

The fact that we are reformers of Judaism does not make us less devoted to it. On the contrary, it is an earnest of our devotion to it. You don't bother to reform what you despise; you just leave it alone. You don't expend time, thought, energy and money on something you don't value. You don't build synagogues and schools, train rabbis and teachers, hold services, organise meetings, produce journals, write books and pamphlets, and perform the countless other tasks involved in conducting an active Jewish communal life, unless you care for Judaism. Still less do you incur hostility and ostracism for its sake, as has often been the experience of

4

Liberal Jews, unless your concern for Judaism is above the ordinary.

The Jewish Religious Union was founded in order to win back for Judaism those who were drifting away from it, to awaken in them a new understanding of their heritage, a new respect for it, a new commitment to it. That remains our aim. Loyalty to Judaism, love, admiration and enthusiasm for it, is what 'turns us on', motivates us, impels us. We believe what we believe, we teach what we teach, and we do what we do, because we endorse the words of the ancient Jewish prayer: 'Happy are we! How good is our portion, and how pleasant our lot, and how beautiful our heritage!' (*Service of the Heart*, p. 263).

2 The Heritage of the Congregation of Jacob

The religious character of Judaism

What then is Judaism? As a first approximation, let us say that it is the heritage of the Jewish people. But we can be more specific. It cannot be their genetic heritage. For the theory that the Jews are a race, first propounded in the 19th century by pseudo-scientific antisemites, is now thoroughly discredited. Already in ancient times, as the Bible testifies, the Israelites were of mixed stock, and since then so much mingling of 'blood' has occurred through intermarriage and proselytism that today's Jews represent a mixture of racial types almost as heterogeneous as humanity as a whole. But if Judaism is not transmitted genetically, it must be transmitted culturally, and we may therefore re-define it as the culture of the Jewish people.

But what kind of a culture is it? A view commonly held nowadays sees it as a national culture, and those who advance it point to what they regard as the national characteristics of the Jewish people: their staunch loyalty to one another and to their people, their preservation of the Hebrew language, their age-old attachment to the land of their forefathers, their longing to return to it and to rebuild there an autonomous Jewish commonwealth, the fulfilment of these hopes through the Zionist movement and the establishment of the State of Israel, and the revival of the Jewish national consciousness which this, in turn, has elicited and strives to promote.

Opposed to this view, at least apparently, is the one which looks upon Judaism as a religious culture. The evidence for it is certainly impressive. For the Jews have traditionally understood themselves as a 'Covenant People', charged by God to perform a special task on His behalf in human history, and this sense of 'mission' has undoubtedly played a major role in their survival against the pressure of rival ideologies. The very name 'Israel', and the biblical account of how Jacob acquired it (Gen. 32:23-33), is indicative of the religious nature of Jewish self-understanding, as are innumerable other biblical passages, such as the designation of Israel as 'this people which I formed for Myself, that they might declare My praise' (Isa. 43:21). Equally emphatic are countless Rabbinic teachings, for instance to the effect that if the Israelites had not accepted the Torah, God would have had no further use for them (Shab. 88a), and the memorable phrase in the prayerbook which describes them as *am ha-m'yachadim sh'mo*, 'the people who proclaim God's Unity' (see, e.g., *Gate of Repentance*, p. 204).

More generally, it may be pointed out that the Jews' literature, which is the chief product of their cultural creativity, is predominantly a religious literature (Bible, Midrash, Talmud, Zohar, etc.); that their leadership has been mostly a religious leadership (priests, prophets, rabbis); that their institutions have been characteristically religious institutions (temples, synagogues, schools); that their calendar has been a religious calendar (sabbaths, holydays, feasts and fasts); and not least, that the only mode of entry into their Community, other than by birth, has been the religious process of conversion.

Until the thirties or forties of this century, these two views were generally considered mutually antagonistic, and the founders of our Movement emphatically espoused the religious one. Indeed, they tended to see in the national view a deplorable attempt to reinstate an antiquated tribalism, and a threat to what they regarded as the purer, nobler, more advanced and mature understanding of Judaism as a universal religion. That was especially true of Dr. Claude Montefiore who, to the end of his life, clung to 'his old ideal

7

of the Englishman of the Jewish faith'. Rabbi Dr. Israel Mattuck, on the other hand, was more conscious of the Jews' peculiar 'solidarity' and therefore insisted on defining them as a 'people of religion', with some emphasis on the word 'people'; and though he opposed both the spirit of Jewish nationalism and the political goals of the Zionist movement, especially as defined in the Biltmore Programme, he took a serious interest in the Middle East conflict, urged moderation on both sides and supported the binational solution of the Ichud movement led by his fellow alumnus of the Hebrew Union College and President of the Hebrew University, Judah L. Magnes. Less typical was his Associate Rabbi, Maurice L. Perlzweig, who was an ardent supporter of Zionism long before that became fashionable in Jewish religious circles, Orthodox or Progressive.

Today we tend to see the issue in a rather different light. Not only have we long since welcomed the establishment of the State of Israel and recognized our obligation to support it, but we are also willing to admit that the totality of Jewish culture includes secular-national elements which we no longer feel obliged puritanically to disown. We are, rather, inclined to say: 'I am a Jew, and consider nothing Jewish alien to me.' Nevertheless, we do re-affirm the conviction of those who founded our Movement that Jewish culture is primarily a religious culture; that Judaism, though not 'only' a religion in any narrow sense, is primarily a religion; that the purpose of Jewish existence is primarily a religious purpose; and that therefore our Movement must remain, as it has always been, primarily a religious movement. In short, we affirm the traditional Jewish view that it is, above all, the Torah which is 'the heritage of the congregation of Jacob' (Deut. 33:4).

3 Sing to the Lord a New Song

The need for reform

To say that we affirm Judaism is not to say that we affirm everything that has been taught in the name of Judaism in the past. That would involve a host of contradictions. For Judaism has not been static through the ages; it has been a dynamic religion, growing and developing. Nor has it ever been monolithic at any one time; there have always been varieties of Judaism. Therefore some selectivity is necessary, and this involves the problem of authority. How Liberal Judaism deals with this problem will be better understood after a brief survey of what preceded it.

In the history of Judaism two major phases must be distinguished: Biblical and Rabbinic. In the Biblical period the foundations were laid: beliefs about God and man, Israel and the nations, past and future, right and wrong; laws about personal righteousness, ritual purity and social justice; a sacred calendar of sabbaths and festivals; and a sacrificial cult performed by a hereditary priesthood in a central sanctuary. The teachers of this period were Moses and the Prophets, who were convinced that God had spoken to them, and instructed the people accordingly, often prefacing their words with a phrase such as 'Thus says the Lord'. Gradually, their teachings were written down in a library of books which became the Bible. All these books were declared sacred, and special sanctity was attached to the Pentateuch, which was regarded as Moses' own account of God's revelations, through him, to the Israelites at Mount Sinai.

9

A new beginning occurred in the 2nd century B.C.E. with the emergence of the Pharisees. They challenged the exclusive authority of the priesthood; developed a non-priestly, non-sacrificial, congregational form of worship, that of the Synagogue; established schools and colleges; and created a new class of lay scholars who later became known as Rabbis. They accepted the Bible, and especially the Pentateuch, which they called the 'Written Torah', as divinely revealed and therefore completely authoritative. But they also believed that it had to be interpreted and supplemented in the light of the so-called 'Oral Torah', a body of additional teachings which, they alleged, had like-wise been revealed by God to Moses but handed down by word of mouth through Joshua, the Elders, the Prophets and the Men of the Great Assembly.

On the basis of this twofold Torah, the Rabbis con-structed a monumental code of conduct for every aspect of life. This part of their activity is called Halachah and is best understood as their attempt to answer authoritatively and in every detail the question, 'What does the Lord your God require of you?' (Deut. 10:12) It gave birth, first to the Mishnah, then to the Talmud, and was further elaborated and systematised in the medieval law-codes, such as the Shulchan Aruch. But the Rabbis also engaged in another activity, called Aggadah, which arose out of their inter-pretation of the Bible (in its non-legal aspects) and produced a great profusion of legends as well as reflections about God and man and Israel and every other non-legal subject under the sun. This material provided the contents of the literature called Midrash; much of it also found its way into the Tal-mud. In this area, unlike the Halachah, the Rabbis did not attempt to achieve agreement or impose uniformity; they gave the imagination free rein and allowed divergent opinions to stand side by side. In striking contrast with the Church Fathers, they laid down what a man must do, not what he must believe. There was only one exception to this rule: the liturgy. For since this was regulated by the

Halachah, the Jewish worshipper became *de facto* committed to the beliefs which it expressed.

Thus, on the foundations laid in Bible times, the Rabbis erected a huge superstructure which is best termed Rabbinic Judaism. The system worked remarkably well for many centuries—until the age of Emancipation. Then it began to lose its hold upon an ever increasing proportion of the Jewish people, who became in varying degree estranged from it and unobservant of its norms. Whose fault was this, the people's or the system's? That was the great question of the time. One party blamed the people. Released from the centrapetal pressures of the Ghetto and exposed to the centrifugal pressures of their new environment, they had become disloyal to their heritage; therefore they must be chided for their laxity and exhorted to return to a life of strict compliance with the Halachah as codified in the Middle Ages. This became known as the Orthodox party.

Others, who became known as the Reform party, maintained that the system had become to some degree antiquated and needed to be revised. At first they merely embellished the Synagogue services and made a few minor concessions to the new conditions in other areas of religious observance. But before long some of them came to perceive that the root of the problem lay deeper, in a crisis of belief. The Middle Ages were over. Scholasticism was dead. There was a new spirit of free inquiry. Philosophy had declared itself independent of theology. Science was advancing. Historians were re-examining the past with the tools of modern, critical scholarship. The Bible itself was studied by these methods and in the context of other ancient Near Eastern civilizations, and many of the traditional assumptions about its veracity and uniqueness, and about the history of its composition, including the Mosaic authorship of the Pentateuch, were called into question.

If many emancipated Jews no longer obeyed all the precepts of Rabbinic Judaism, it was not only because the new social circumstances made it difficult to carry them out;

it was also because the new intellectual climate raised doubts about their divinely revealed origin, and hence about their obligatoriness. In short, the whole basis of authority of Rabbinic Judaism had begun to crumble and needed to be reconsidered. The second phase in the history of Judaism was coming to an end, a third phase would have to be initiated. It would of course draw heavily on the two preceding phases, but it would not be identical with either. The new Judaism would be in many respects, even in most respects, similar to the old, but it would be based on a different concept of authority.

Not all the Reformers saw the problem in this light, and to this day many of them speak and write as if the passing of the Middle Ages had left the foundations of Rabbinic Judaism entirely intact, so that it is only necessary to make a few slight alterations to the superstructure, to give it a little 'cosmetic treatment'. That has not been the approach of our Movement, which has rather seen it as its task to re-examine, and where necessary reconstruct, Judaism, as it were, from the foundations upwards. And though on a number of specific issues we have moved some way from the radicalism of our founders towards a more conservative posture, that is still where we stand. We affirm, therefore, that the question, 'What does the Lord your God require of you?', remains the central question, but we can no longer automatically assume that the old answers are in all respects still valid. We have to ask the question anew, studying reverently what the past has said about it, learning from it all we can, even giving it the benefit of any doubt, but nevertheless with a forthright openness of mind towards considerations drawn from contemporary knowledge, thought and circumstances which may sometimes point to a different conclusion. We affirm that the modern age demands a modern form of Judaism; that the vast transformation which the world has undergone since the close of the Middle Ages makes it imperative that we should respond to the challenge to 'sing to the Lord a new song'.

4 The Seal of God

The need for intellectual integrity

The implications of Liberal Judaism's standpoint for the practice of Judaism will be explored later. Here our main concern is with the theory of Judaism. And in this area, it might be thought, there should be no serious problems since, as we have seen, Judaism has not historically subjected belief to the straitjacket of an official creed. That statement, however, requires one or two qualifications. For one thing, as we have already remarked, the traditional Jewish liturgy, which is regulated by the Halachah, expresses in its prayers some fairly definite doctrines which, by reciting them, the worshipper is presumably expected to affirm. Indeed, the very response 'Amen' expresses such an affirmation. Furthermore, that same liturgy has for several centuries included a brief summary of Maimonides' 'Thirteen Principles of the Faith', and this fact has given them a quasi-official status.

More generally, the whole structure of Rabbinic Judaism presupposes a belief in the divine authority of the Torah which is always implied even when not stated. And, just occasionally, it is explicitly affirmed. The Mishnah, for instance, mentions, among those who 'have no share in the world to come', the person who says that 'the Torah is not from Heaven'. This statement, which provided the point of departure for Maimonides' Thirteen Principles, is quite atypical of the Mishnah, which is otherwise concerned to define correct practice, not correct belief, and should be seen as a relic of an ancient controversy, with polemical exaggeration for emphasis. Nevertheless, it has exerted considerable influence.

In particular, the doctrine it asserts, that the Torah is from Heaven (*torah min ha-shamayim*), has become the watchword of Orthodox Judaism. As typical of this may be taken the following remark by a 19th-century Chief Rabbi of Posen: 'Only he can be considered a conforming Jew who believes that the divine law book, the Torah, together with all the interpretations and explanations found in the Talmud, was given by God himself to Moses on Mount Sinai to be delivered to the Jews and to be observed by them for ever'. Thus the term 'Orthodox', which is on the whole inapplicable to traditional Judaism, since it regulates conduct rather than belief and is therefore an 'Orthopraxy' rather than an 'Orthodoxy', turns out to be, after all, accurately descriptive of the prevailing trend among its latter-day exponents.

Moreover, the doctrine of the divinity of the Torah has far-reaching implications. For it commits the person who subscribes to it, not merely to a particular view of Revelation, but to the contents, in every detail, of a whole literature. He must then believe that whatever the Torah asserts is true, and that whatever it commands correctly expresses God's will. This view is commonly called fundamentalism. In fairness, however, it needs to be pointed out that the fundamentalism of Orthodox Judaism is not to be equated with that of certain Christian sects. It is not literalist. It allows scope for interpretation. But in so far as the interpretation, in its turn, has become fixed by tradition, that has its own authority. It would therefore be correct to say that Orthodox Judaism asserts the divine authority of the Torah as traditionally interpreted.

Thus Rabbinic Judaism, even in its classical form, and especially in the more rigid form of its modern Orthodox interpretation, imposes on the individual's freedom of belief many more restrictions than is immediately apparent. To us, as Liberal Jews, these restrictions are unacceptable. For if the adjective in 'Liberal Judaism' stands for anything, it stands for freedom. This freedom has both positive and negative implications. It is both a 'freedom for' and a 'freedom from'. Its positive sense is that we wish to be free to believe what seems true to us and to do what seems right to us. But in order that this may be, we must be free from the stranglehold of the dogmas of past ages.

What is at issue here is nothing less than intellectual integrity, which demands that the search for truth should be unfettered. Of course it is right that we should listen humbly and reverently to the wisdom of others, past and present, and especially to the wisdom of our own Jewish tradition, which is immense; that we should expose ourselves to its influence, immerse ourselves in its spirit, and give it every opportunity to persuade us, to mould our thinking, to elicit from us insights which we might otherwise have failed to attain. But in the last resort our own minds must give—or withhold —their assent. For it can never be right to affirm that which, when we have made every effort to learn from the past and present, and to be honest with ourselves, seems to us certainly, or even probably, false.

To say this is not to question the integrity of others. All through the centuries, from the age of the Pharisees to the age of Emancipation, it was possible to believe with perfect sincerity in the divinity of the Torah and the other doctrines of Rabbinic Judaism, and no doubt most Jews did so, for they had no compelling reason to do otherwise. And the same applies to countless truly Orthodox Jews today, since they conscientiously reject those tendencies in modern thought and knowledge which are at variance with Rabbinic Judaism and are therefore still able, to that extent, to give their sincere assent to the mental outlook of the Middle Ages. But for the great majority of today's Jews that is no longer possible. They must therefore either ignore the problem or re-think their Jewish beliefs. To us the latter alternative seems the only honourable one.

The spirit of Liberal Judaism is therefore a spirit of truth-seeking, and it was never better expressed than by Claude

Montefiore in a sermon he preached at one of the early services of the Jewish Religious Union: 'Truth . . . is not the best loved of the virtues; and yet it is one of the noblest, as it is, perhaps, the hardest of them all. It needs courage and resolution and strength of will: it must be loved for its own sake, or it will not be practised . . . There can be no truth which is not Divine, there can be no falsehood which is Divine . . . If any doctrine of religion is in conflict with an ascertained law of science, that doctrine cannot be true; therefore it cannot be religious. It is no longer religious to believe it; it is, on the contrary, irreligious, for God is true, and the source of truth. If the statements in the sacred books of any religion are in antagonism with the proved doctrines of science, those statements are erroneous: held in good faith till science showed their error, they can no longer be held in good faith when science has proved them false . . . There is no truth which is not God's truth, and there is no truth which at the last shall not prevail. "Great is truth, and mighty above all things" (Apocrypha, I Esdras 4:35) . . . The divorce between officialism and truth is becoming greater in each decade . . . Specious arguments are used about not disturbing the innocent faith of uneducated persons, about preserving unity in Judaism, about not making bad blood, about letting sleeping dogs lie, about letting error destroy itself, about the urgent practical questions which beset and menace the community, about the sovereign virtue of peace, about the immense need of outward forms, about the needful illusions in the education of children, about all things under heaven except one. And that one omitted argument or subject is: What do we owe to truth?'

We endorse that spirit. For all the great loyalty which, as we constantly emphasize, Jews owe to their Tradition, greater still is the loyalty they owe to Truth. For those Jews who live mentally, as well as physically, in the modern world, a gap has arisen between Tradition and Truth. We see it as our task to close that gap, so that they may again be able to believe and practise their religion with sincere devotion. And we regard that as a religious and a Jewish undertaking, for we affirm the great saying of the Talmud, *chotamo shel ha-kadosh baruch hu emet*, that 'the seal of the Holy One, blessed by He, is Truth' (Yoma 69b, Shab. 55a, Sanh. 64a).

5 The Beginning of Wisdom

The existence of God

At the core of Judaism stands the affirmation of God. It is the unifying principle which holds the whole edifice together. It is presupposed by almost every Jewish concept and precept. It is asserted, explicitly or implicitly, on almost every page of Jewish literature. To our ancestors it seemed so certain that they supposed only a fool able to say, 'There is no God' (Psalms 14:1, 53:2), and so fundamental that they could declare, 'The fear of the Lord is the beginning of wisdom' (Psalm 111:10, Prov. 1:7). To most Jews through the ages it was a conviction so firmly held that they would have been willing to die for it, as many did.

Can we affirm it? Does our loyalty to truth permit us to do so? It must be frankly confessed that for many people the belief in God has become more difficult in recent decades. The founders of our Movement—Lily Montagu, Claude Montefiore, Israel Mattuck—could have been described, as Spinoza once was, as 'God-intoxicated'. Such intensity of faith is rare today. Even those who continue to believe in God will often admit that the degree of assurance has diminished.

The causes of the decline are not difficult to identify. They include the impact of science, which has not only cast doubt on the veracity of some Bible narratives, but discouraged belief in the supernatural and fostered a general scepticism towards all inherited dogmas. They include the triumph of technology, which has given man an inflated sense of his own power that leaves little room for reverence, and accelerated

18

the tempo of life to an extent that leaves little time for contemplation. They include the all-pervading materialism of our age, which tends to blind us to the reality of the spiritual. They include the influence of atheistic ideologies, such as Marxism, and of positivistic tendencies in contemporary philosophy which deny the very meaningfulness of the proposition that God exists. And they include, not least, the terrible catastrophes of our century, above all the Holocaust, which have persuaded many people that God must be either evil or impotent, and since neither seems likely, to pronounce Him 'dead'.

It is therefore necessary to raise the question: What is a Jew to do if he finds himself unable to believe in God? We would urge him not, on that account, to disown his heritage or dissociate himself from his community. For though the God-concept is basic and central to it, Judaism does possess other merits. Even if there were no God, the history of the Jewish people would still be an inspiring history, the literature of Judaism would still be a noble literature, and above all Judaism's ethical teachings would retain their intrinsic validity and their vital importance for the enhancement of human behaviour and the amelioration of human society.

Beyond that, we would beg him not to close his mind. Since the affirmation of God, if true, would be the most fundamental of all truths, we would suggest to him that he should continue to wrestle with it, as Jacob wrestled with the angel, for the sake of the blessing to be won. We would invite him to ponder yet again the evidences that have in the past prompted human beings to affirm the reality of God: the wonders of nature, the miracle of life, the insistence of the conscience, the progression of history, the testimony of prophets and sages, mystics and saints. We would advise him to expose himself to religion by studying its literature, witnessing its activities and seeking contact with persons who possess the indefinable but unmistakable quality of 'spirituality'.

We would also remind him that not all present trends point away from religious belief. On the contrary, there is, not least among the young, a growing disenchantment with materialism and an increasing concern with the quality of life, a dawning sense of the sterility of a soulless rationalism, a reviving suspicion that 'there are more things in heaven and earth . . .', a renewed yearning for that apprehension of the Transcendent which the East seems to have preserved better than the West.

We affirm the reality of God, but in full awareness, not only of the particular difficulties which such an affirmation presents for many people at the present time, but also of the essential mystery which must always surround the Godhead, since our human minds are too puny to grasp its fulness. Therefore we feel that in the spiritual aspects of our congregational life there must be an emphasis on seeking, on reaching out, rather than an over-confident asserting of having found, and that we must speak about God, and to Him, with a certain diffidence, tentativeness and allusiveness. At least the modern elements in our liturgy must acknowledge that we live in what Martin Buber once called an 'eclipse of God' and express a longing that the eclipse may pass rather than an assurance that it has done so already. The following examples may illustrate what we mean:

'May we learn to overcome doubt, endure anxiety, and bear pain bravely, that with hearts and minds less troubled, we may come closer to You and to our fellow-men.' (*Service of the Heart*, p. 85f.)

'Dimly we have seen a vision; fitfully we have felt a presence; and faintly heard a voice not ours. The blazing stars, particles too small to see, the mind reaching out, the smile of children, the eyes of lovers, melody filling the soul, a flood of joy surprising the heart, a helping hand, the apprehension of mystery at the core of the plainest things—all these tell us that we are not alone. They reveal to us God, the vision that steadies and sustains us.' (*Service of the Heart*, p. 93)

'We are children of a time which has sought to dethrone You. We have proclaimed Your death and said to the works of man: you are our gods. Strange then to see the emptiness Your absence has brought upon us! Strange that the agonies of our time grow more numerous and more intense, the more our worship centres on ourselves. Strange that we grow smaller without You, smaller without our fathers' humble faith. Scarcely do we tremble before You . . . May this day which yet holds us in its spell, bring us back to You . . .' (*Gate of Repentance*, p. 73).

> 'God of pity and love, return to this earth.
> Go not so far away, leaving us to evil.
> Return, O Lord, return. Come with the day.
> Come with the light, that men may see once more
> Across this earth's uncomfortable floor
> The kindly path, the old and loving way.
> Let us not die of evil in the night.
> Let there be God again. Let their be light.'

We do not know all the answers, but we invite our fellow Jews to seek them with us, to engage with us in a common search, so that we may together endeavour to recapture, in so far as it has faded, the vision of God. The knowledge of God is an aspiration never fully attained. But the 'fear of the Lord', in the sense of the humble, reverent, open-minded, open-hearted longing to experience Him—that is 'the beginning of wisdom'.

6 Our God and our Fathers' God

The Jewish conception of God

Although there is a sense in which God must remain for ever 'beyond our finding out', Judaism has consistently made a number of definite affirmations about His nature, and these, with only minor qualifications, Liberal Judaism has always endorsed. First and foremost among them is the Unity of God as emphasized throughout Jewish literature and pre-eminently in the Shema, which is recited with special solemnity in our Services: 'Hear, O Israel, the Lord is our God, the Lord is One'. This Unity is both an extrinsic one, denying a plurality of deities, as in the pagan religions, and an intrinsic one, excluding the concept of a multiple God-head, as in Christianity. Its implications are immense, for from it follow the unity of the cosmos, which is the funda-mental presupposition of the entire scientific enterprise, and the unity of mankind, which we shall discuss further in a later chapter.

More precisely, the unity of the cosmos derives, not only from the fact that God is One, but that He is its Creator. This too we affirm, though we do not pretend to know how God created the universe. The Biblical Creation Story is obviously a myth. To say this is not to disparage it. Myths can be very valuable, and the Biblical Creation Myth is perhaps the greatest of them all. To take the details of it as factual would be a mistake, not only because they are in some respects contradicted by modern cosmology, and not only because the author could not have had any means of knowing the facts, but because they were always intended poetically; it would be a misunderstanding of what a myth *is*. But the general principle affirmed by the story remains valid independently of the details. (A modern Creation Myth might make use of the currently favoured 'Big Bang' theory, which, incidentally, would accord well with the Jewish emphasis that God created the world by an act of will or command, that is, by a sudden outpouring of creative energy. Cf. the Psalm verse, 'By the word of the Lord the heavens were made, and all the host of them by the breath of his mouth' (Psalm 33:6), the first verse of the Adon Olam which declares that 'all things were made by His will' (*Service of the Heart*, p. 371), and the frequent Rabbinic designation of God as *mi she-amar v'hayah ha-olam*, 'He who spoke, and the world came into being'.)

Judaism further affirms that, having created the universe, God continues to guide and sustain it; that, as an ancient Jewish prayer puts it, 'in His goodness He renews the work of creation continually, day by day' (*Service of the Heart*, p. 39). In particular, God rules the world through what we have come to understand as the laws of nature. What then about miracles? If the word is understood in its literal sense, as happenings which evoke wonder, there is no difficulty. In that sense the world is full of miracles, as acknowledged in the old Jewish prayer in which we thank God 'for the miracles that are with us day by day' (*Service of the Heart*, p. 53). But does God sometimes produce 'special effects' which are not merely extraordinary but actually involve a suspension or modification or reversal of natural law? That seems hard to credit, or to reconcile with the belief in an all-wise, unchanging God. Accordingly, the rationalists among the Jewish philosophers, such as Maimonides, have done their best to 'explain away' the miracles of the Bible as accounts of dreams or, failing that, as pre-ordained at the time of Creation. For us the problem is less serious since we are in any case inclined to see in these stories a large element of legend. But the question whether, in principle, supernatural miracles can occur, remains. Montefiore and

Mattuck thought not. We are inclined to think likewise, but less categorically—to keep a slightly more open mind on the subject.

A major element in the Jewish conception of God is its emphasis on His transcendence. This really follows from the belief in Him as Creator, for as such He must necessarily be different from, and greater than, the universe which He created. He is therefore not to be identified with the universe —which would be pantheism—or with any part of it, whether mineral, vegetable, animal or human, this being the basic fallacy of paganism which the Hebrew Prophets strove so hard to dispel (a criticism which would appear to apply also to the Christian doctrine of the Incarnation). This is why Judaism has always been so intransigently opposed to idolatry, as in the Second Commandment.

Perhaps the classic statement of the doctrine of God's transcendence is the declaration of the Prophet of the Exile: 'My thoughts are not your thoughts, neither are My ways your ways, says the Lord. For as the heavens are higher than the earth, so are My ways higher than your ways, and My thoughts than your thoughts' (Isa. 55:8f). One aspect of it is that God is incorporeal, so that all references to Him in human terms, known as anthropomorphisms, must be understood as strictly metaphorical, a fact on which Maimonides, among others, laid great stress. Two other aspects are God's omnipotence and omniscience. Both of these raise difficulties which we shall take up at another point, but for our present purpose it is sufficient to affirm that God is far exalted in power and wisdom above man and any other being.

Closely related to God's transcendence is His eternity. 'Before the mountains were born, or earth and universe brought forth, from eternity to eternity You are God. For a thousand years in Your sight are but as yesterday when it is past, or as a watch in the night.' So says the 90th Psalm. And the Adon Olam declares that, as God existed before the world, so He will exist when it has ceased to be. Furthermore, as He is independent of time, so He is independent of space; He is omnipresent. 'Whither shall I go from Your spirit? Whither shall I flee from Your presence? If I ascend to the heavens, You are there! If I make my home in the lowest depths, behold, You are there!' So says the 139th Psalm, and the Rabbis emphasized that there is no place devoid of God's presence (see, e.g., *Service of the Heart*, p. 224).

Uncompromising though Judaism is in its insistence on God's transcendence, it also affirms the converse: His immanence. This is the great paradox which lies at the heart of the Jewish conception of God and which is the theme of the Adon Olam. In one sense, His omnipresence provides the link, for the Psalm just quoted continues: 'If I take up the wings of the morning and dwell on ocean's farthest shore, even there Your hand shall lead me, Your right hand shall hold me'. So, too, the Bible assures us: 'In every place where I cause My name to be remembered, I will come to you and bless you' (Ex. 20:21). God *cares* for human persons and allows them to enter into a relationship with Him. It is, moreover, a two-way relationship. God addresses man in revelation, and man addresses God in prayer. 'The Lord is near to all who call upon Him, to all who call upon Him in truth' (Psalm 145:18). About both aspects we shall have more to say later.

More generally, God guides the whole historic process. He is not only the Lord of Nature; He is also the Lord of history. This is one of the major distinctions between Him and the pagan nature deities, and explains why Judaism strove so strenuously to transform the Canaanite nature feasts into celebrations of historical events, such as the Exodus from Egypt.

It is particularly in the context of God's immanence that we find ourselves compelled to use anthropomorphic terms: He cares, He speaks, He hears, He sees. We therefore need to remind ourselves again that they are only metaphors. Today, more perhaps than in the past, people tend to fight shy of such metaphors, even to deny that they believe in a 'personal'

25

God. But most of them nevertheless feel it right to refer to God as 'He' rather than as 'It'. They may therefore admit that, since the human being is the highest phenomenon within the universe known to us, it is more appropriate to think of God in human than in sub-human terms, for instance as a physical force, and that the concept of a 'personal' God, although a metaphor, is therefore nevertheless the best metaphor available to us.

What makes it seem appropriate to think of God as 'personal' is above all Judaism's conviction that He is to be understood as a moral God. In this lies the great chasm that divides him from the pagan deities, who were amoral when they were not immoral. To describe this aspect of God's nature, Judaism uses many terms. One which stands on its own is 'holiness', for it alludes at once to His transcendence and to His moral perfection, as well as to the awe which both arouse in the beholder. Another general designation is 'righteousness'. This comprises justice on the one hand, love and mercy on the other. Between these two aspects there is a certain tension, but no contradiction. Judaism has generally held them in balance, perhaps with slightly greater stress on the latter. Especially relevant is the passage known in Jewish tradition as 'The Thirteen Attributes of God' which is recited with great solemnity on the High Holy Days: 'The Lord, the Lord God is merciful and gracious, endlessly patient, loving and true, showing mercy to thousands, forgiving iniquity, transgression and sin, and acquitting'. Attention may also be drawn to the common Rabbinic appellation of God as *ha-rachaman*, 'The Merciful One'.

The significance of attributing these moral qualities to God is twofold: that they inhere in Him, so that He rules the world in accordance with them, and that they define the nature of the demands He makes on those who would worship Him. About both aspects we shall have more to say.

Meanwhile our brief sketch of the Jewish conception of God has, we hope, shown sufficiently that in this, the most fundamental area of Jewish belief, we stand essentially where

26

Jews have always stood. The principal Jewish prayer, the Tefillah, begins: 'We praise You, O Lord our God and God of our fathers' (*Service of the Heart*, p. 44). A famous comment on these words makes the point that it is not sufficient to acknowledge the God of our ancestors: we must also discover Him anew for ourselves. We endorse that statement. Every Jew, in every generation, must seek God both in the tradition he has inherited and in his own thought and experience. To our minds, these two approaches present no serious discrepancies. In all essentials, the God of our fathers is also our God.

7 A Little Less Than Divine

The Jewish conception of man

'What is man?' asks the 8th Psalm, and it answers: 'You have made him little less than divine'. A more familiar rendering is: 'A little lower than the angels.' If that is the meaning, it may remind us that angels feature fairly prominently in Jewish folklore. To what extent former generations seriously entertained the belief in their existence is debatable, but it may be safely assumed that few Jews do so today. The case against it is partly the absence of evidence for it and partly the fact that the clarity of the distinction which Judaism normally makes between God and man would become somewhat blurred by the interposition of a class of 'celestial' beings between them. Accordingly, the founders of our Movement omitted the references to angels from the liturgy, and though it is no longer likely that they would be taken as anything other than poetic fancy, we can see no good reason for restoring them.

In any case, it is pretty clear that the 8th Psalm alludes to the Creation Story, which mentions no angels but declares that God created man in His own image (Gen. 1-26f, 5:1). Whatever this may mean precisely, it points to the exalted status Judaism accords to man in the divine scheme. To us it means that within the universe, at least as far as it is known to us, man is the highest creature. His intelligence, inquisitiveness, memory, imagination and creativity; his ability to speak and write and transmit culture; his ever-growing mastery over his environment; his self-consciousness and his sense of truth and beauty—in all these respects he is vastly superior to all other animals and therefore more 'Godlike' than they.

Of the many implications commonly drawn from this doctrine, two require fuller discussion in this chapter. (A third will be discussed in the next chapter, and a fourth in Chapter 13). The first of these is that man possesses free will. There have indeed been Jewish philosophers who have denied this; but they have been the exception, not the rule. Certainly the classical sources of Judaism seem to presuppose that man is free to choose, especially between good and evil. Sometimes, indeed, this is emphatically asserted, as in the words of Deuteronomy, 'I call heaven and earth to witness against you this day, that I have set before you life and death, blessing and curse; therefore choose life' (Deut. 30:19), and in the saying of the Rabbis that 'everything is in the hand of God except the fear of God' (Ber. 33b, Meg. 25a, Nid. 16b). Whatever may be the philosophical difficulties inherent in this view (and they are probably no greater than those posed by its denial), on a common-sense level it is of the utmost importance to maintain it, for moral exhortations would lose their point if the freedom to choose were not real.

It does, however, raise a problem about a supposed attribute of God to which we have alluded earlier: His omniscience. For if human beings are really free, how can God know in advance what they will do? Perhaps the resolution of the paradox lies in the thought that the human distinction between past and future does not exist for God, and perhaps that is what Rabbi Akiva meant when he grasped both horns of the dilemma with his famous dictum, 'All is foreseen, yet freedom is given' (Avot 3:16). But if the conflict is genuinely irreconcilable, then, rather than deny human free will, we should be inclined to question God's foreknowledge and be prepared, to that extent, to qualify the traditional understanding of His omniscience.

In addition to asserting that man is free to choose between right and wrong, Judaism has traditionally taught that his fundamental predisposition is towards the former. This

29

would indeed seem to be a necessary consequence of the belief that he was created in God's image. In the words of an ancient Jewish prayer, 'The soul which You have given me, O God, is pure, for You created it, formed it, and breathed it into me' (*Service of the Heart*, p. 141). That man is basically good, is implied in countless Jewish teachings and epitomized in the Rabbinic doctrine of the *Yetzer Tov*, the 'Good Inclination'.

But the more we emphasise this doctrine, the more the problem of evil stares us in the face. The problem falls into two parts of which the first really belongs to a previous chapter (but we thought it would be more convenient to deal with it here), for it refers to those evils, or seeming evils, in the world which are not of man's making and which therefore raise questions about the nature of God: the cruelty among animals and the diseases and natural disasters which befall human beings, apparently indiscriminately. Why does God cause or permit them? Either, it would seem, He cannot prevent them, in which case He is not all-powerful, or He does not desire to prevent them, in which case He is not all-good. This is indeed the most serious problem for theism, and it would be idle to pretend that we possessed a wholly satisfactory answer. Of course Judaism has wrestled with it and proposed many partial solutions. One of them is to the effect that suffering is sometimes for man's benefit—the Rabbinic doctrine of *yissurin shel ahavah*, 'chastisements of love'. Another, which we shall discuss presently, suggests that the injustices of this world will be rectified in another. We may also surmise that a world governed by unchanging laws is better than any logically possible alternative, and that these laws, even if they are the best, will unavoidably sometimes produce phenomena hurtful to individuals; or else, that an evolving universe is preferable to a static one, and that the 'natural evils' are, so to speak, the unavoidable 'teething troubles' of an evolving universe. But in the end we must still confess, with Job, our ignorance and say, in the words of an ancient rabbi, that 'it is beyond our power to explain the prosperity of the wicked or the suffering of the righteous' (Avot 4:15). If we continue to affirm God, it is not because, with Him, the world makes perfect sense to us, but that without Him it would make less sense, or even no sense at all.

But one point needs to be added: that if we were compelled to choose between God's omnipotence and His benevolence, our inclination would be to sacrifice the former in order to maintain the latter. For the concept of a non-benevolent God is intolerable, whereas the concept of a less-than-omnipotent or not-yet-omnipotent God (which has indeed been proposed by some theologians) seems a possibility which would leave the major thrust of religion intact.

The other part of the problem, and in some ways the graver one, is posed, not by these 'natural' evils but by those which human beings inflict on one another. This, in its turn, is twofold: Why do they act in these ways, and why does God permit them to do so? In answer to the second question —unless, once again, we take refuge in the concept of a non-omnipotent God—we can only speculate that perhaps the preservation of human free will is to God of such immense importance that it overrides all the cruelties which result from its abuse, and that we should therefore envisage 'a compassionate, torn and sorrowing God who gave us free will out of love, and having forbidden himself to interfere, must behold in agony what we do with our freedom'.

If that is correct, then it is man rather than God who needs to be arraigned for such catastrophes as the Holocaust. Why do human beings perpetrate such barbarities? Is it that they are sometimes under the control of a supernatural evil power? Judaism has on the whole resisted the temptation to believe that; it leads easily to the heresy of dualism, which Judaism has consistently condemned. It is true that Satan, originally only an accusing angel, came to be regarded as an evil being; but he belongs to Jewish folklore rather than theological doctrine, and the occasional reference to him in the liturgy has been removed from the prayerbooks of Liberal Judaism

31

(*Service of the Heart*, Note 46, p. 469). Most Jews would concur with Joseph Conrad's remark that 'the belief in a supernatural source of evil is not necessary; men alone are quite capable of every wickedness'.

But how is that fact to be explained? Rabbinic Judaism accounts for it by the doctrine of the *Yetzer ha-Ra*, the 'Evil Inclination'. This, however, is not evil in itself; it is rather an umbrella term for those basic drives in man which, because they are self-regarding, and because they are so powerful, often impel him, if they are not controlled, to disregard the rights, interests and feelings of his fellow men and so to act in ways hurtful to them—especially his desires for pleasure, power and property. In themselves, however, these drives are good. As the Rabbis said, 'If it were not for the Evil Inclination, no man would build a house, marry, beget children or engage in business' (Gen. Rabbah 9:7). If this analysis of human evil in terms of selfishness seemed adequate in the past, it is harder to be satisfied with it after witnessing the horrors of the Holocaust. To account for the darker side of human nature, which has been revealed to us so appallingly in the present century, we need to add something more. There is, it seems, a certain rebelliousness in man which is perhaps basically a resentment of the authority of a Higher Being and therefore an aspect of human self-assertion. And there are in man aggressive and sadistic tendencies which, in severe cases, and when stirred up by vicious propaganda and mass hysteria, can lead to extreme brutality. But if these conditions are essentially pathological, then we can adhere to the traditional Jewish view that in his normal state man desires good rather than evil. And in these days of widespread pessimism about human nature, to uphold that view, both in spite of and because of all we have suffered, may well be one of Judaism's major contributions to civilization.

Whatever the causes of human sin, there is always a remedy available. It is the way of *Teshuvah*, 'Return'. As Montefiore wrote, 'To us there is but one atonement—the atonement wrought by human repentance and the divine forgiveness; by God's grace and help on the one hand, by human remorse and effort on the other. The process is doubtless very subtle, but put into words it is simple, and in practice it is efficacious and works. That is the Jewish atonement: we know no other'. Here, too, we stand where Judaism has always stood.

8 The End of Days

The hope for a Messianic Age

The affirmation that man was created in God's image raises the further question whether he shares his Creator's immortality. The ancient Biblical view of the human being as a body animated by the divine 'breath of life' (see, e.g., Gen. 2:7), did not lend itself readily to such a belief. Rather, it was supposed that the dead fell into a perpetual sleep in an underworld called Sheol. Nevertheless, the thought that it might be possible to re-awaken them was entertained, as is shown by the story of the woman of En-Dor who raised the spirit of Samuel (I Sam. 28); and if that belief was generally suppressed, it was probably on account of its association with pagan doctrines and superstititions. By the time of Ezekiel it had gained ground; hence his use of the resurrection *motif* as a metaphor for the national revival of the Jewish people (Ezek. 37:1-14). And in the book of Daniel it is already a firm expectation that at some future time 'many of those who sleep in the dust shall awake' (Dan. 12:2). This doctrine of a future bodily resurrection was, moreover, espoused by the Pharisees, against the opposition of the Sadducees, and written into the Jewish liturgy, especially the second benediction of the *Tefillah* which affirms that God will 'revive the dead'.

About the same time, probably under the influence of Greek thought with its matter-spirit dualism, the idea began to be contemplated that the soul might survive independently of the body. An early instance of this, though one which seems to assume that the soul loses its individuality, may be

34

found in Ecclesiastes: 'The dust returns to the earth as it was, but the spirit returns to God who gave it' (Eccles. 12:7). A belief in a more personal immortality came to the fore in the wake of the Maccabean wars, when the martyrdom of so many brave young men seemed to demand that there should be another world in which the injustices of this one could be redressed (see, e.g., II Maccabees 7:9, 23). It found expression, for instance, in the Apocryphal passage which declares that 'the souls of the righteous are in the hand of God, and no evil shall touch them . . . To the foolish they seem to have died . . . But they are at peace . . . and their hope is full of immortality' (*Wisdom of Solomon*, 3:1-4), and in the Rabbinic teaching that 'this world is only a vestibule before the world to come; prepare yourself in the vestibule, that you may enter into the hall' (Avot 4:16).

In Rabbinic literature as a whole, both these beliefs—in the ultimate resurrection of the dead, and in the translation of the soul, upon the death of the body, into the spiritual realm of 'the world to come'—are frequently asserted, exist side by side, and cannot always be easily disentangled from one another. Liberal Judaism, from its inception, denied the former but affirmed the latter. That the doctrine of the bodily resurrection on earth of the dead of all generations (or at least of those who have 'passed muster') defies reason, is too obvious to require argument. Accordingly, Liberal Judaism has deleted, re-worded or re-interpreted the liturgical references to it. For most modern Jews the only serious issue is whether the belief in a spiritual immortality can be upheld. The founders of our Movement were confident of it, though even they made some allowance for doubt, so far as the liturgy is concerned, by speaking of 'the hope of immortality' rather than asserting it categorically. Today, while some Liberal Jews believe as firmly as ever in an afterlife, many are unsure about it, and some frankly sceptical; and this fact is reflected, as it needs to be, in the tentativeness on the subject of our current liturgy.

While there have been, and are, various views about the

ultimate destiny of the individual human being, Judaism has been consistently optimistic about the ultimate destiny of mankind as a whole. A time will come, it has taught, when all nations will recognise and worship the true God, and obey His will, and therefore live together in brotherhood and peace. 'All the nations whom You have made shall come and bow down before You, O Lord, and honour Your name' (Psalm 86:9). 'The Lord shall be King over all the earth; on that day the Lord shall be One, and His name One' (Zech. 14:9). 'It shall come to pass at the end of days that the mountain of the Lord's house shall be established as the highest mountain, and raised above the hills; and all the nations shall flow to it, and many peoples shall come and say: "Come, let us go up to the mountain of the Lord, to the house of the God of Jacob, that He may teach us of His ways, and that we may walk in His paths." For out of Zion shall go forth God's teaching, and the word of the Lord from Jerusalem . . . And they shall beat their swords into plough-shares, and their spears into pruning-hooks; nation shall not lift up sword against nation, neither shall they learn war any more' (Isa. 2:1-4). 'And they shall sit every man under his vine and under his fig-tree, and none shall make them afraid' (Mic. 4:4).

Along with this universal hope, Judaism has also cherished a narrower, national one. This evolved gradually out of the longing that the Jewish people—divided, misruled, con-quered and dispersed—might be re-united under an exemplary ruler of the royal house of David, who became known as the Messiah, that is, the Anointed One. This hope grew in intensity under the oppressive rule of Rome, and gave rise to an increasingly elaborate, fantastic and super-natural vision of the final drama of history, involving the ingathering of the exiles, the overthrow of the forces of darkness under their mythical kings Gog and Magog by the forces of light, the triumphant reign of the Messiah-King, the Day of Judgment and the Resurrection of the Dead. Such speculation flourished particularly among peripheral Jewish

36

sects, such as the Essenes, and found expression in a new type of prophecy called apocalypse. (It was this which provided the background of the movement associated with Jesus of Nazareth.) However, the Pharisees too, though they discouraged its more extravagant forms, went along with it up to a point, and wrote it into the Jewish liturgy; and after the *debacle* of 70 C.E. it became further associated with the hope for the rebuilding of the Temple.

Liberal Jews are inclined to dismiss this whole eschatology as a web of escapist fantasies, and to endorse, rather, the sober judgment of the greatest Babylonian Amora, Rav: 'All the predicted ends have already passed; now all depends on repentance and good deeds' (Sanh. 97b). That is to say, they affirm the hope for a 'messianic' age in the broad sense of the redemption of mankind, but they do not believe that it will come about suddenly, dramatically, miraculously, supernaturally, through the agency of one individual (the Messiah), but slowly, gradually, progressively, through the spiritual strivings, moral exertions and social reforms of all men and nations. And they object especially strongly to the hope for the restoration of the Temple and its sacrificial cult, which, in their view, would be a preposterous retrogression.

Accordingly, they have deleted, or appropriately modified, all affirmations of this ancient eschatology, as well as reminiscences of the sacrificial cult, in the liturgy. We believe, moreover, that our view in this matter is shared by the great majority of today's Jews, including many who belong to Orthodox synagogues, and it is therefore a source of perpetual puzzlement to us how they are able to reconcile it with their integrity to recite such prayers as the following: 'On account of our sins we were exiled from our land, and removed far from our country, and we are unable to go up in order to appear and prostrate ourselves before thee, and to fulfil our obligations in thy chosen house, that great and holy temple which was called by thy name . . . May it be thy will . . . that thou mayest again in thine abundant compassion have mercy upon us and upon thy sanctuary, and mayest

37

rebuild it . . . Bring our scattered ones among the nations near unto thee, and gather our dispersed from the ends of the earth. Lead us with exultation unto Zion thy city, and unto Jerusalem the place of thy sanctuary with everlasting joy; and there we will prepare before thee the offerings that are obligatory for us . . .'

The hope we affirm is at once more rational and grander. It is the universal hope expressed in such prayers as these: 'Trusting in You, O Lord our God, we hope soon to behold the glory of Your might, when false gods shall cease to take Your place in the hearts of men, and the world will be perfected under Your unchallenged rule; when all mankind will call upon Your name and, forsaking evil, turn to You alone . . . Then the Lord shall be King over all the earth; on that day the Lord shall be One, and His name One' (*Service of the Heart*, p. 365f). 'O Lord our God, teach all Your works to stand in awe before You, and let all creatures tremble at Your presence. Let all life revere You, and all creation turn to You in worship. Let all become a single fellowship to do Your will with a perfect heart . . . Then the just shall see and rejoice, the upright be glad, and the faithful sing for joy. Violence shall rage no more, and evil shall vanish like smoke; the rule of tyranny shall pass away from the earth, and You alone, O Lord, shall have dominion over all Your works' (*Gate of Repentance*, p. 27f).

9 A Light to the Nations

The mission of the Jewish people

To the Reformers of the 19th century, and to the founders of our Movement, not the least objectionable feature of the old eschatology was its 'geopolitical' aspect: the hope for the ultimate return of all Jews to their land of origin, there to re-establish an autonomous commonwealth. For this seemed to contradict their whole understanding of the historic role and destiny of the Jewish people. Since, however, just this hope has been partially fulfilled in our lifetime, we need to clarify where we now stand in regard to it.

We believe that the Israelites were chosen by God to perform a special role in the drama of human history. Why they were chosen, is a matter of speculation. Perhaps simply because they responded to God's call, which is the import of the well-known Midrash that He offered it to all nations, but that they alone accepted it, saying: 'We will do and obey'.

They accepted the responsibility not only on their own behalf, but on behalf of all their future generations (see, e.g., Deut. 29:13-14). This explains why Jewish status is transmitted from parents to children. In this sense the Jews are, unlike the Christian Church, a 'natural community'. Nevertheless, what is transmitted from generation to generation is, as we said in Chapter 2, a cultural heritage. As such, it can be renounced (by the apostate) and espoused (by the proselyte).

The only problematic case is that of the children of a mixed marriage. The Rabbis ruled that they follow the mother (Kid. 3:12). Liberal Judaism, however, regards this as a mistaken policy, based on an unwarranted interpretation of a Scriptural passage (Kid. 68b, interpreting Deut. 7:2) and presumably motivated by the extraneous consideration that maternity is easier to prove than paternity, if not also by the false as well as irrelevant supposition that children have a closer biological affinity with their mother than with their father. Accordingly, Liberal Judaism regards religious upbringing as the deciding factor in such cases.

We may therefore define a Jew as a person who for any of three reasons—Jewish parentage on both sides, Jewish parentage on one side plus Jewish upbringing, or conversion —has become a recipient of the Jewish heritage and, not having renounced it, is subject to the obligations which it imposes. To the extent to which he fulfils these obligations, he is a good Jew; to the extent to which he fails to do so, he is a bad Jew; in either case he is a Jew and shares in the collective responsibility of the Jewish people.

We regard that responsibility as a religious one, and to be discharged not only for the Jews' own benefit, but for the benefit of mankind. 'It is too small a task that you should be My servant only to raise up the tribes of Jacob and to restore the survivors of Israel; I will make you a light to the nations, that My salvation may reach to the end of the earth' (Isa. 49:6). It is, indeed, nothing less than to play a leading role in the movement of human history towards its consummation in the 'messianic age'—or, which is another way of saying the same thing, the establishment of the Kingdom of God.

What must we do to fulfil this task? First, we must survive, for without Jews there is no Judaism and no Jewish contribution to civilization. We therefore consider it an ineluctable duty to ensure the survival of the Jewish people by combating antisemitism and aiding Jewish refugees. This is one reason why we welcome the establishment of the State of Israel as a haven of refuge for persecuted Jews, and acknowledge our obligation to enable it to continue to perform that function, as well as our obligation to support other 'rescue operations', such as that on behalf of Soviet Jewry.

But physical survival is not enough, for we can perform our appointed task only if we remain loyal to our heritage, and especially to our religious heritage. We therefore see it as our duty to combat assimilation—in the sense of the abandonment or diminution of Jewish religious identity— and to discourage mixed marriages in so far as they are likely to have such consequences. But by the same token we oppose the secularising tendencies in Jewish nationalism which relegate the Jewish religion to the status of a peripheral and optional element in the 'Jewish national culture'.

Loyalty to Judaism means the practice of the high standards which it demands, chiefly *lishmah*, for its own sake, but also as an example to others. The ideal is nothing less than that we should be 'a kingdom of priests and a holy nation' (Ex. 19:6); and in the words of Morris Joseph, 'A kingdom of priests implies something more than a people leading a consecrated, but self-contained life. It means a people whose holiness, travelling beyond the national confines, shall help to consecrate mankind. A priest presupposes a congregation, and a kingdom of priests a world to minister to'.

Does this ministry require us to teach by precept as well as example? And should we therefore proselytise? It is a historical fact that 'the Pharisees and Rabbis were eager for converts, highly successful in winning them, and friendly in their treatment of them'. It is also a historical fact that when the Christian Church became triumphant, it used its power to forbid and prevent Jewish proselytism and that, as a result, Jews tended to make a virtue out of necessity and persuade themeslves that Judaism does not desire proselytes. It is indeed true that according to Rabbinic doctrine Gentiles are only required to observe the 'Seven Laws of the Descendants of Noah' and are therefore under no 'obligation' to become Jewish. But from this is does not follow that it may not be in many cases to their spiritual advantage (and to that of their spouses and children, if they marry into the Jewish community). To cherish Judaism, yet not to feel any desire to share its treasures with others, is at best inconsistent. To maintain that it can only be of benefit to born Jews, is a manifest absurdity.

Liberal Judaism has generally been favourably disposed towards the acceptance of converts, and its present attitude is best summed up in the ancient Rabbinic saying: 'The gates are open at all times, and whoever wishes to enter may enter' (Ex. Rabbah 19:4). We do not think it right to bring any pressure, even the slightest, on individual Gentiles to become Jewish; our experience of Christian missionary activity has made us very sensitive to the resentment that can cause and the harm it can do. But we do think it right to make available to them the opportunity to find out about Judaism, and, if it commends itself to them so strongly that they seek conversion of their own accord, to be as welcoming and helpful to them as we can, provided only that they are sincere and that they are willing to satisfy all essential requirements, in particular to undergo a course of instruction sufficient to equip them adequately to lead a Jewish life.

It remains only to consider the locale in which the destiny of the Jewish people is to be enacted. Historically, it has vacillated between Eretz Yisrael and the Diaspora. Sometimes one has been the more populous, creative and influential centre, sometimes the other. That has depended largely on external factors, but partly also on the Jews' voluntary choice of domicile. For their dispersion from their homeland during the Greco-Roman period was by no means wholly an enforced one. As David Polish has pointed out, 'the homing impulse in Judaism is counterbalanced by an almost equally powerful centrifugal force'. For most Jews during the last 2,000 years the 'Return to Zion' has been only an eschatological dream. But the persistence of antisemitism in Christendom, and its resurgence even after the Emancipation had promised better things, finally combined with other factors to spur the Zionist movement to translate the dream into reality.

We have already said (on pages 8 and 40) that we welcome the establishment of the State of Israel. We do so because it has provided a refuge for hundreds of thousands of Jews displaced by the horrors of the Holocaust and by conditions of persecution or insecurity in Arab and Communist lands, and because these experiences have convinced us of the urgent need, which seemingly only a sovereign Jewish State can satisfy, that there shall be at least one country in the world whose doors are open by right to any Jew seeking admission. We welcome it also because it makes possible a form of Jewish life different from, and in some respects preferable to, that of the Diaspora. To a remarkable extent, that possibility has already been fulfilled, and we look forward to its further fulfilment. The inspiration of the land itself, because of its natural beauty and historical associations; the revival of the Hebrew language and the emergence of a neo-Hebrew culture; the intensive study of Jewish literature in the country's academic institutions; the opportunity to apply Jewish values to social policy and state-craft, and to contribute to the economic advancement of the Middle East as a whole—all these are aspects of the great promise inherent in the State of Israel and persuade us of our duty to lend it support in all appropriate ways, including the encouragement of those Diaspora Jews who, attracted by the challenge, may wish to settle there.

There is, however, another side which cannot be ignored. The domination of Israel's life by Secular Nationalism on the one hand and an antiquated Orthodoxy on the other does not bode well for its spiritual future. Neither does the discrimination still practised against the country's small but growing Progressive Jewish movement owing to the political influence of the National Religious Party. The bloody conflict between the State of Israel and its Arab neighbours has been a tragic, though unintended, consequence of its establishment. And the nature of international *Realpolitik* is such that the Israeli Government may sometimes find itself, or believe itself to be, compelled to act in ways which do not

43

exemplify the highest ideals of Judaism or convey the most favourable image of the Jewish people to the world at large.

It must also be said that the tendency of some Zionists to speak of Aliyah as the only honourable option open to Jews, and to disparage Jewish life outside the Land of Israel as abnormal, unsatisfactory and impermanent, cannot but undermine the self-respect and self-confidence, and in the long run the vigour, of the Diaspora communities. It is also, in our view, unwise on more general pragmatic grounds, for the State of Israel itself needs a strong Diaspora, and the precarious and unpredictable political future of the Middle East, as of other parts of the world, strongly suggests that it would be foolish, as it were, to put all the eggs of Jewish survival into one basket; indeed, that the Jews' dispersion is a factor positively favouring their survival. In addition, to assert that Judaism can be fully or properly lived in only one country of the world is to belittle its universal character and potential, of which we remain profoundly convinced.

Therefore we cannot endorse the hope for the *total* 'ingathering of the exiles', either as a short-term or as a long-term objective, for we envisage for Judaism a grander destiny. To that extent we stand where the founders of our Movement stood. We differ from them, however, because we see positive value in the *partial* 'ingathering of the exiles' which has occurred since. The truth of the matter, as we see it, is that each of the two foci of Jewish life, Israel and the Diaspora, has its own strengths and weaknesses, advantages and temptations, opportunities and difficulties, and that they therefore have different but complementary roles to play in the fulfilment of the Jewish people's responsibility and destiny.

10 The Word of the Lord

The progressive nature of Revelation

Whatever may be the ultimate goal of Jewish history, the immediate task of the individual Jew is to live in conformity with God's will. But is God's will known? Rabbinic Judaism answers: 'Yes. It is known because God has revealed it to us.' How then does Rabbinic Judaism see the process of Revelation? Briefly, as follows.

First, God made known certain basic laws of behaviour to the ancestors of the human race, such as Adam and Noah. Then He enjoined certain additional precepts upon the ancestors of the Jewish people, that is to say, the Patriarchs. Finally, the process was completed at Mount Sinai. There, amidst thunder and lightning, God proclaimed the Ten Commandments to the assembled Israelites, then revealed the rest of the Torah to Moses. Some of it he wrote down at God's dictation; this became the 'Written Torah', comprising 613 commandments as well as the surrounding narratives, together making up the Pentateuch. The rest he committed to memory and handed down by word of mouth; this became the 'Oral Torah' which was ultimately recorded in the Mishnah and the subsequent Rabbinic literature.

With this, the process of revelation was essentially at an end, for the Prophets who appeared after Moses only re-inforced what had already been revealed at Sinai, and exhorted the people to obey it; they did not add anything substantially new to it. Nevertheless, the books of the Prophets, and indeed all the remaining books of the Hebrew Bible, are also entirely trustworthy, for they were all written

45

under the guidance of the 'holy spirit' (*ruach ha-kodesh*); therefore, in a broader than the usual sense, they too may be called 'Torah'.

After Haggai, Zechariah and Malachi, prophecy ceased (see, e.g., Tosefta, Sotah 13:12). Therefore any books known to have been written after that time, or otherwise lacking the marks of divine inspiration, were excluded from the canon of 'Holy Scripture'. It was forbidden to read them publicly, and they became known as 'extraneous' or 'hidden' books or 'Apocrypha'. The exact line of demarcation was, however, long debated and not finally settled until the 2nd century C.E., the books of Ecclesiastes, Esther and the Song of Songs having been among the disputed cases (see, e.g., Shab. 12b, Yad. 3:5, Meg. 7a).

Although prophecy had ceased, individuals might still on occasion hear a Divine Voice (*Bat Kol*) or experience some other manifestation of God's Presence (*Gillui Shechinah*), but they no longer received any new revelations of Torah for the guidance of the people as a whole. The further elucidation of God's will became from now on a matter of applying human reason to the already existing records and traditions of the twofold (Written and Oral) Torah. It was this process which produced the Mishnah and Talmud, and thereafter the Responsa, Codes and Commentaries. Indeed, the process has never ceased; it continues still. But it was inevitable that the Torah, on its legal side (Halachah), should become increasingly 'frozen' from age to age. For as more and more outstanding questions were authoritatively settled, so the area in which there was still fluidity naturally shrank and became confined to ever more peripheral and trivial details. Since the 16th century, when Joseph Caro wrote his definitive Shulchan Aruch, the Halachah has been almost entirely rigid.

This Rabbinic view of the process of Revelation went virtually unchallenged all through the Middle Ages, and Orthodox Judaism maintains it still—indeed, it is its indispensable basis. Therefore, for an Orthodox Jew, any question as to God's will is always susceptible of a clear and definite answer; it is merely a matter of looking up the Shulchan Aruch, or, if he is in any doubt, of asking an Orthodox Rabbi, who will himself consult the literature of the Halachah.

In modern times, however, this view has sustained a series of lethal blows. To begin with, Bible scholars have demonstrated beyond reasonable doubt that the Pentateuch is a composite work, embodying at least four distinct written sources, all of them centuries later than Moses, though based on antecedent oral traditions which may in some instances go back to the time of Moses and even remoter antiquity. They have also demonstrated that the Bible as a whole enshrines a great diversity of traditions, reflecting different stages in the development of Hebrew law and thought as well as different views and attitudes on the part of individual writers; in short, that throughout the Biblical period Judaism was never static but always in a state of flux. And they have demonstrated, further, that it did not exist in hermetically sealed isolation from the rest of the world, but interacted with other Near-Eastern cultures and was greatly influenced by their myths and legends, laws and customs, sometimes adopting them, sometimes adapting them, sometimes reacting against them.

Seen from this vantage-point, the Bible is not a single book but a whole library, a literature spanning over a thousand years, which derives its unity, not from any monolithic internal consistency as to detail, but from the grand general themes which run through it: the history of a people in search of God, its loyalty and disloyalty to its Covenant with Him, its self-awareness and self-criticism, its recollections of its past and its hopes for its future and for the future of humanity as a whole.

This view does not deny the unsurpassed greatness of the Bible, either as literature or as religious literature. It has indeed rendered untenable the traditional belief that every one of its statements and commandments is a verbatim account of a supernatural revelation; but by demonstrating that its numerous authors were human beings, children of their age and products of the social and cultural milieu of the ancient Near East, it has made all the more impressive the fact that in so many respects they transcended these limitations to propound ideas far ahead of their time and even of timeless validity.

At the beginning of the present century this view of the Bible was already well established among scholars. But in the world of organized religion, both Jewish and Christian, it was still fiercely contested. The founders of our Movement were sharply attacked for espousing it; Chief Rabbi Dr. Joseph H. Hertz polemicized against it; and even the Rabbis of England's Reform Synagogues maintained in those days a non-committal silence on such controversial issues as the authorship of the Pentateuch. Since then, however, the situation has changed dramatically. When Rabbi Dr. Louis Jacobs published *We Have Reason To Believe* (1957) and other books frankly accepting the modern critical approach to the Bible, the storm of protest, though it caused a furore at the time, soon died down; and the publication in 1972 of the monumental *Encyclopaedia Judaica* has shown that nowadays practically all academically respectable Jewish Bible scholars, both in Israel and in the Diaspora, accept the modern view as a matter of course. In other words, the 'heresy' of our founders has been abundantly vindicated.

But it is one thing to accept the modern view and another to perceive its religious implications. It is the abiding achievement of Claude Montefiore that he was the first Jew in this country to wrestle seriously with this problem, and though not all his conclusions remain wholly valid, the broad outlines do. A restatement of them which seems acceptable to us would be as follows.

The writers of the Bible were human—nobly human but not super-human. They were inspired by God; but there can be no guarantee that they were so inspired in everything they wrote. Moreover, even when they were so inspired, we

48

cannot assume that they always understood and recorded correctly what God said to them; for though 'the word of the Lord is pure' (Psalm 18:31), it does not necessarily retain its pristine purity when it filters through the human mind of the prophet who first interprets it and then expresses it in the language of his culture. Thus, to quote Louis Jacobs, the Bible 'contains a human as well as a divine element' and there is 'error as well as truth' in the record of revelation.

But if the Bible is not as infallible as was formerly thought, then the distinction between it and other literatures becomes less categorical. There is, for instance, no reason to ascribe inerrancy to those who fixed the canon, and it is possible to hold that some apocryphal books (such as Ben Sira) may have greater religious value than some biblical books. Indeed, it becomes necessary to question the dogma that at a certain point in time prophecy ceased. No doubt the forms of religious experience and expression changed, but surely there have always been individuals—and not only among Jews—whose spirit was touched by the spirit of God. And that applies to the Rabbis, too, even though they were too humble to put it that way. For their development of the religion of the Bible—sometimes because of and sometimes in spite of their belief in its infallibility—shows many advances which reflect a keener religious perceptiveness or a higher ethical sensitivity and which may therefore very well be attributable to divine inspiration.

Judaism, in short, has always been a developing religion. To say this is not to say that it has always developed at the same rate or in the most desirable direction. There have been outstandingly dynamic and creative periods, such as the age of Moses, the age of the Prophets and the age of the Pharisees and Rabbis, and there have been other periods when the energies of the Jewish people were devoted mainly to consolidation and preservation, so that there was little progress and sometimes even retrogression. But always, or nearly always, there has been some advance; there have been individuals who, standing on the shoulders of their predecessors, have seen a little further; and if, as we believe, such growth in religious knowledge is to be attributed, not only to the human search for God, but also to God's response to it, then we may speak of 'Progressive Revelation'.

This view is grander than the traditional one because, instead of asserting that God has revealed Himself only in one time and place, it affirms that He has revealed Himself in many times and places; indeed, that the dual, inseparably interlinked process of man's quest for God and God's self-disclosure to man is, potentially at least, a continuous one. But though it is the grander concept, the guidance it yields is of necessity less definite. On many issues it leaves room for doubt; the question, 'Did God really say . . . ?', can never be by-passed.

The will of God is no less decisive for Liberal Jews than it is for Orthodox Jews. The question on which they differ is only how far it is knowable. That it is knowable with complete assurance, as regards all that human beings need to know, is a medieval view which cannot be sustained in the light of modern knowledge. It would make the religious enterprise a great deal easier (though also less adventurous) if it were true; but we know that it is not. There is no escape from the predicament of human fallibility—not even, let it be added, for the fundamentalist, for his acceptance of the traditional view of the inerrancy of Scripture is itself a human and therefore fallible decision, and one which, if erroneous, carries countless other errors in its train. To fundamentalists it seems scandalous that liberals should question the veracity of a single Scriptural verse; to liberals it seems no less scandalous that fundamentalists should impute to God teachings which reflect all too plainly the human limitations of a particular period of history. To fundamentalists for instance, it is a kind of blasphemy to deny that God commanded Saul to slaughter the Amalekites (I Sam. 15); to liberals it is a kind of blasphemy to *assert* that He did.

It may be regrettable, but it must be accepted as a fact, that we do not possess a manual of divine revelation which is guaranteed to contain 'the truth, the whole truth and nothing but the truth'. All we possess is the written record of the *strivings* of human beings—especially the prophets and sages of Israel—to understand and interpret God's will. From that record we must learn all we can. We must not glibly dismiss it in the light of contemporary fashions of thought which may prove to be only ephemeral. For those who speak to us out of the Jewish past were in many cases giants of the spirit whom the present cannot equal. We should therefore listen to their words with humility and reverence, and give them every opportunity to influence and persuade us. Nevertheless, we may not close our minds to other considerations: the developing trends in Judaism itself, historically understood; the assured conclusions of modern knowledge; the promptings of our own consciences; the circumstances of contemporary life; the needs of our present-day communities. There is no neat and tidy formula by which the will of God can be determined for every situation. We must draw guidance from all relevant sources, and let the answers emerge from the interplay between them. Sometimes the answers will seem certain, sometimes only probable, and sometimes problematic. It is not a foolproof method, but it is the best method available to us. All we claim for it is that by it we are more likely to approximate to the truth than by any other.

11 What does the Lord your God require of you?

The sovereignty of God's will

What are the implications of this modern, historical, reverent yet not uncritical approach to the classical sources of Judaism? The question falls into two parts: belief and practice. So far as belief is concerned, our guiding principle, as we said in Chapter 4, must be truth. Of course, as we also said in that chapter, our perception of truth must be based on knowledge. In particular, we must study the classical sources of Judaism and give them every opportunity to teach us what they can. But in the last resort we must decide for ourselves what we can and what we cannot honestly believe. Happily, as we pointed out in Chapter 3, Judaism has always conceded a large measure of individual freedom in this area of Aggadah, as distinct from Halachah. Therefore, in so far as we find it necessary to modify some beliefs which former generations of Jews saw no cause to question, we merely make ampler use than they found it necessary to do of a freedom which Judaism has always granted in principle. Therefore no serious problems arise, except in so far as belief 'spills over' into practice, as in the matter of liturgy, to which we shall return.

But before we move on from belief to practice, let us raise the general question: Which is more important? There is no doubt that Judaism (unlike Christianity) has characteristically been more concerned that human beings should act rightly than that they should believe rightly. A striking example of this is afforded by a Midrash which tells us that the generation of the Flood were destroyed because, though they acknowledged God, they were steeped in robbery, whereas the generation of the Tower of Babel were only scattered because, though they defied God, they loved one another (Gen. Rabbah 38:6). Even more startling is a passage in the Palestinian Talmud which attributes to God the words: 'Would that they would forsake Me but observe My Torah' (J. Chag. 1:7).

It is nevertheless true, of course, that belief influences, because it motivates, action. Consequently we do find in Judaism considerable stress on right motives. The ideal is that we should always act out of love (Sifrey to Deut. 6:5) rather than fear or for the sake of reward (Avot 1:3), and that all our deeds should be done 'for the sake of Heaven' (Avot 2:12). A favourite saying of the Rabbis was that 'it matters not whether you do much or little, as long as your heart is directed to Heaven' (Ber. 17a). That religious acts should be performed with the correct intention (*Kavvanah*) is always urged and sometimes declared essential. None the less, right conduct remains obligatory even when the right motive is absent. Moreover, he who habitually acts in accordance with God's will, even if initially he does so from lower motives, is likely to find himself ultimately doing so from higher motives. As the Rabbis put it, *mittoch she-lo lishmah ba lishmah*, 'Having at first performed a commandment from ulterior motives, a man will come to perform it for its own sake' (Pes. 50b).

Closely related to the issue of belief versus action is that of the relative importance of study and action. This, too, has been much debated. Opinions range from that of Rabban Gamaliel I who said, 'Not study but practice is the chief thing' (Avot 1:17), to the famous saying of the Mishnah which, after listing some of the highest moral obligations, delivers the punch-line that 'the study of Torah is equal to them all' (*talmud torah k'neged kullam*). But even this seemingly exaggerated statement must be understood to mean that the study of Torah is so important because it teaches right conduct. That, too, is the conclusion of a debate recorded in the Talmud between Rabbi Tarfon, who opined that action is more important than study, and Rabbi Akiva, who asserted the opposite, when the majority sided with Akiva on the ground that 'study leads to action' (Kid. 40b).

All necessary qualifications having been made, it therefore remains true that, as has so often been said, Judaism is a religion of deed rather than creed, and the 14th-century Jewish philosopher, Chasdai Crescas, summed up the essence of the matter when he said that in Judaism 'salvation is attained, not by subscription to metaphysical dogmas, but solely by love of God expressed in action. That is the cardinal truth of Judaism' (Or Adonai II 6:1).

How then should we act? From a religious point of view that means: How does God require us to act? The two questions are identical. About that Liberal Jews and Orthodox Jews are in perfect agreement. They differ only about the extent to which God's will is knowable. Orthodox Jews believe that it is not only knowable but known, that all the necessary information is contained in the Torah and its traditional interpretation, that is, in the literature of the Halachah. But they believe this on the basis of a conception of Revelation which, though tenable until the close of the Middle Ages, is, as Liberal Jews believe, no longer tenable.

From a Liberal Jewish point of view, therefore, God's will is not always knowable with complete assurance, and the process of trying to discover what it is is anything but simple. Of course it involves consulting the Bible. But there is no guarantee that its authors always understood correctly what God requires. Therefore the authority of the Bible is only presumptive, not conclusive; it guides us but does not necessarily govern us.

Of course we need to consult also the post-Biblical Jewish literature, showing how the teachings of the Bible were interpreted, amplified and developed in the course of Jewish tradition, especially by the Rabbis. But the Rabbis too were human and fallible. Often they were right *because* they believed in the Bible, so that they studied it 'with a magnifying glass', became suffused with its spirit, and drew many valid inferences from its teachings. Sometimes they were right *in spite of* their belief in the Bible, consciously or unconsciously bringing to bear upon its interpretation their own ethical insights and sensitivities, which were not infrequently in advance of those of the Biblical writers: (One of many instances of this is that they legislated out of existence the Deuteronomic law ordaining the death penalty for the 'stubborn and rebellious son'.) Sometimes they were misled by their belief in the inerrancy of the Bible into perpetuating an antiquated law which their conscience would not otherwise have inclined them to uphold, and sometimes they were misguided by the prejudices of their own age and milieu. (Among the latter may be instanced the disabilities they imposed on women, sometimes without being compelled to do so by the Scriptural text.) Therefore the Rabbinic literature, too, can have for us only a presumptive, not a conclusive authority.

In addition, we consider it necessary to take into account modern knowledge. This includes the historical study of the Bible, Talmud, etc., themselves, indeed of the whole historical development of Judaism, which can often throw light on why a particular period legislated as it did, and this in turn can often help us to judge how much or how little weight should be given to the law in question. It includes also such disciplines as sociology, psychology and medicine whose modern insights, unavailable to the Jewish legislators of former generations, are sometimes very relevant to the issues they dealt with.

Finally, we need to consult our own consciences. Indeed, in the last resort that must be the decisive consideration, for, in an important sense, it can never be right to act against the conscience, or wrong to act in accordance with it. Of course, what we take to be conscience may in reality be only prejudice or predilection. Therefore caution is necessary. As Claude Montefiore used to emphasise, we must be guided by our *educated* conscience. And since we can never be sure

55

that our conscience is sufficiently educated, therefore this source of guidance, too, cannot in practice be regarded as infallible.

How then are decisions to be reached as to what God requires of us? Liberal Judaism would say: By bringing into play all the factors we have mentioned—the teachings of the Bible; their interpretation in Jewish tradition; the historical study of the entire development of Judaism; the insights to be gained from modern scientific knowledge regarding man and nature; and the conscience of the individual. It is a complex process, but there is no short cut; and, as we said at the conclusion of the previous chapter, the results it yields will not always seem certain; sometimes they will seem only probable, and sometimes (as on some aspects of such problems as abortion and euthanasia) we may find ourselves obliged to say in all honesty: 'We wish we knew what God's will is, but we don't.'

From this it follows, too, that not all Liberal Jews will necessarily reach the same conclusion on every issue. And therefore we feel that we should refrain from legislating (as distinct from giving guidance) where it is not necessary to do so. That applies, in our view, to all matters of private practice. In this area coercion is in any case impossible. We believe that it is also inappropriate. Therefore we extend to the area of private practice the same kind of freedom which Judaism has traditionally granted in the area of private belief. That is, the individual must act according to his conscience. But once again, we stress that it must be an educated conscience. And since not all individuals are equally educated, equally acquainted with the sources of Judaism, and therefore equally competent to weigh up all relevant considerations, therefore we think it right and necessary that guidance should be given by those (in practice this tends to mean the rabbis) who may be assumed to be more highly qualified than others in these respects. Exactly how detailed and definite the guidance should be remains, as it always has been, a matter of dispute among Liberal Jews.

But all would agree that there is such a need, and in practice a good deal of such guidance is given in the published books, prayerbooks and pamphlets of Liberal Judaism, as well as conveyed orally in sermons, lectures, study-groups and the like.

There is, however, also such a thing as public practice. For religion has a communal, as well as an individual, dimension. And in this wider sphere it is manifestly impossible that every person should do what is right in his own eyes. It is of the nature of a community, even a liberal community, that it needs to have communal rules. In our Movement every Congregation is autonomous, and its rules (for instance, as to how its Services shall be conducted) are determined by its democratically elected Council under the guidance of its Rabbi. But there are also matters in which, by common consent, it is necessary or at least desirable that the various constituent Congregations of the Union of Liberal and Progressive Synagogues should forgo the exercise of their autonomy and voluntarily agree to abide by common policies. This applies, for instance, to most aspects of personal status, conversion, marriage and burial. In these matters the decision-making body is the Union of Liberal and Progressive Synagogues, specifically its Rabbinic Conference.

Thus, in Liberal Judaism, religious practice is a subject both of guidance (where it affects only the individual) and of legislation (where it affects the community). In either case it emerges from the consensus of the religious leadership, after careful study and consideration of all the relevant factors mentioned above. Moreover, it is of the essence of Liberal Judaism that whatever guidance or legislation is issued should always remain subject to revision in the light of new, or previously overlooked or inadequately assessed, circumstances and insights.

In so far as one can speak of a Liberal Jewish Halachah, that is its nature. It is not identical with the traditional, Rabbinic Halachah, though it has a great deal in common with it, both in general and in countless details. Above all, it is completely at one with the traditional Halachah in affirming that on all issues the fundamental question to be answered is: 'What does the Lord your God require of you?' (Deut. 10:12).

12 These are the things which you shall do

The priority of right conduct

As we have seen, Liberal Judaism, in its approach to religious practice, deals with each issue on its merits, in the light of all the relevant considerations, ranging from the teachings of the Bible to the promptings of the contemporary conscience, and then issues guidance—or, where necessary, legislation—on the basis of the consensus of its religious leadership. Since this process has now been going on for 75 years in our Movement, it is to be expected that, whatever differences of opinion may remain on points of detail, certain generally agreed principles will have become crystallized. That is indeed the case, and in this chapter and the next we shall discuss a few of them.

The first, which we have already touched upon more than once, is the principle of integrity. While this applies more obviously to matters of belief, it also has practical implications, particularly, as we have previously pointed out, in the area of liturgy. It would manifestly be wrong to require Liberal Jews (or anybody else!) to affirm in their prayers, either in their homes or in their synagogues, beliefs which they cannot reasonably be expected to regard as true. That is why we have revised the traditional Jewish liturgy so as to eliminate from it any affirmations, explicit or implicit, of beliefs which we consider antiquated and no longer tenable, for instance concerning angels, Satan, miracles, the personal Messiah, the total Ingathering of the Exiles, the rebuilding of the Temple, the restoration of the sacrificial cult, and the Resurrection of the Dead. But if that seems like a negative, though necessary, reform, it should be added that our prayerbooks also contain a good deal of innovation in the positive sense, in that they embody much material from ancient and modern Jewish sources which had not previously been utilized liturgically, as well as many newly written prayers and meditations voicing thoughts, sentiments and hopes which receive little or no expression in the traditional Jewish liturgy.

It is, however, not sufficient that the prayers we recite should be doctrinally acceptable; it is also essential that they should be understood. And not only in a vague and general sort of way. Unless the worshipper is fully aware of the meaning of every sentence he utters, his worship lacks integrity. Some Jews know Hebrew so well that they are able to pray in Hebrew with such full comprehension. For the great majority of our members that is not true; and though we do all we can to encourage the learning of Hebrew by children and adults, we must be realistic and say that it is not likely to become true. Therefore it is manifestly necessary that our Services should be conducted to a large extent in the vernacular. It would be necessary even if the Halachah disallowed it. Fortunately, that is not the case, for the entire halachic literature, from the Mishnah (Sotah 7:1) to the Shulchan Aruch (Orach Chayyim 62:2, 101:4), explicitly permits it.

So overwhelming, indeed, is the case for the use of the vernacular in Jewish worship that it is the continued use of Hebrew which needs to be justified. But the case for that is also strong. It includes the fact that Hebrew is the language in which the classical Jewish liturgy was largely composed, and that no translation can fully convey all its meanings and nuances; that its use helps worshippers to become familiar with it and encourages them to learn it; and that it maintains a bond between Jews of all lands, whatever their mother tongue may be. We are inclined to give rather more weight to these considerations than did the founders of our Movement, and therefore the amount of Hebrew used in our synagogues has tended to increase somewhat in recent decades. The exact proportion of Hebrew to English varies from Congregation to Congregation according to the preferences of its leaders and their assessment of the level of Hebrew knowledge among the members.

But while prayers verbalize beliefs, other rituals symbolize them, and therefore the principle of integrity applies to them as well. For instance, the special privileges still accorded in Orthodox synagogues to *Cohanim* (those allegedly descended from the ancient priestly families) imply the belief that one day the Temple will be rebuilt and the *Cohanim* will then again be required to offer sacrifices. Since we reject that belief, we have abolished the special privileges. (We have done so also because we attach positive value to the principle of the equality of all Israelites before God which is otherwise so laudably characteristic of Judaism and which these privileges infringe.) Similarly, to give only one other example, the prohibition of cremation, which Orthodox Judaism maintains, is bound up with the belief in the Resurrection of the Dead. Since we do not hold that belief, and since none of the other reasons for the prohibition seem to us to have any cogency, we permit cremation.

It should be added that sometimes a ritual can be reinterpreted. What was at one time done for one reason, may subsequently be done for another. For instance, the Bar-Mitzvah ceremony, which formerly celebrated a boy's attainment of his legal majority, may now be understood as marking a stage in the process of his religious maturation. Again, the fast of Tish'ah b'Av, which in the past commemorated primarily the destruction of the Temple, may be observed in memory of other events of Jewish history, such as the Nazi Holocaust, which seem to modern Jews more tragic. Wherever such reinterpretation is possible, we consider it seriously. But there are limits beyond which the connection between the old meaning and the new, or the nature of the symbol and that which it is supposed to symbolize, becomes too tenuous and the principle of integrity is eroded. As such a judgment involves imponderables, not all will agree precisely where the limits lie. But all agree that they exist and that, when they have been reached, the ritual itself must be modified or, where even that is impossible, abandoned.

The second general principle we should like to mention is justice. How greatly this is stressed, both as an attribute of God and as an obligation upon man, throughout the entire Jewish literature, from the Bible onwards, is too well known to require elaboration. It would not be too much to say that it suffuses Judaism. One would therefore expect the particular institutions of Jewish law and ritual to conform to it; and on the whole, that is indeed the case. But there are some exceptions. We have already mentioned the special privileges of the *Cohanim*, a relic of an ancient caste system (Kid. 4:1) which even the Pharisees, in spite of their general egalitarianism, failed to eliminate. But that is a relatively minor instance. More serious is the Biblical law forbidding a *Mamzer* to 'enter the congregation of the Lord' (Deut. 23:3) which the Rabbis interpreted to mean that a child born of an incestuous or adulterous union (a 'bastard' in that sense) may not marry a Jewish person of 'untainted' stock. Since it is plainly unjust to penalize children for the sins of their parents—a principle which the Bible itself acknowledges (Deut. 24:16, Ezek. 18)—Liberal Judaism has abrogated this law. (It is true that such injustices occur in nature; but it cannot be right to add to them in the name of a man-made law. That Orthodox Jews regard it as a divinely ordained law, admittedly puts a different complexion on the matter from their point of view, but not from ours.)

Equally unjust, and more far-reaching in its consequences, is the discrimination against women in traditional Judaism. While their status in Biblical times was in some respects relatively high, as evidenced by the fact that they could become Judges, Prophetesses and Queens, and while in some respects the Rabbis raised their status further, in other respects they legislated to their disadvantage. Thus they

62

disqualified women from serving as judges or witnesses. They permitted men to marry several wives, but not vice versa; and though polygamy was ultimately abolished in the Middle Ages, the earlier phase of the law continued, and continues, to produce injustices. They understood marriage as an act by which the husband 'acquired' the wife, who was only required to give her consent, and made the bride's role in the marriage ceremony a purely passive one. They maintained the one-sided Biblical definition of adultery as intercourse between a man, married or unmarried, and another man's wife. They made divorce a unilateral act (admittedly, with many safeguards for the wife) in which the husband 'dismisses' the wife, not vice versa. They also exempted women from all *Mitzvot* (religious duties) involving a time-factor; and though this was intended as a concession to them, in practice it tended to be taken to mean that they were debarred from performing the rituals in question.

Additionally, they exempted women from the *Mitzvah* of *Talmud Torah*, that is, of receiving or imparting religious education; and since this, too, came to be regarded virtually as a prohibition, Jewish women were generally illiterate from Talmudic until modern times. (This is one of the few inequalities which most Orthodox Jewish communities, following the unacknowledged example of Progressive Judaism, have rectified.) For all these reasons, as well as others, women were generally excluded, at least from about the 12th century onwards, from any active participation in synagogue worship, as is still the case in Orthodox Judaism.

Liberal Judaism maintains that men and women, though not alike (Heaven forbid!), are entitled to equal rights as human beings and members of the Jewish people as 'a kingdom of priests and a holy nation' (Ex. 19:6). This seems to us a self-evident principle of elementary justice. It could have been inferred many centuries ago from the Biblical statement that 'God created man in His own image . . . male and female He created them' (Gen. 1:27). All the sadder does it seem to us that Orthodox Judaism has still not

63

acknowledged it and therefore, in this respect, fallen behind the progress of an increasingly large section of mankind. Liberal Judaism acknowledged it from its inception and has granted women full equality with men both in marriage law and in synagogue life and worship. It is noteworthy that one of the founders of the Jewish Religious Union was a woman, Lily Montagu, and that a woman graduate of the Leo Baeck College is now the Rabbi of one of its Congregations.

The third generally agreed principle is what one might call the primacy of ethics. It follows from the Jewish conception of God, with its emphasis on His moral nature, that what He chiefly requires of those who would worship Him is right conduct rather than the performance of rituals. Indeed, this insight is one of those which most markedly distinguished Judaism from the pagan religions of antiquity. The Prophets hammered it home. 'I hate, I despise your feasts, and I take no delight in your solemn assemblies . . . But let justice roll down like waters, and righteousness like an ever-flowing stream' (Amos 5:21-24). 'For I desire love and not sacrifices, and the knowledge of God rather than burnt offerings' (Hosea 6:6). 'What to me is the multitude of your sacrifices? says the Lord . . . Wash yourselves; make yourselves clean; remove the evil of your conduct from before My eyes; cease to do evil, learn to do good; seek justice, correct oppression; defend the fatherless, plead for the widow' (Isa. 1:11-17). 'Will the Lord be pleased with thousands of rams, with tens of thousands of rivers of oil? . . . He has shown you, O man, what is good; and what does the Lord require of you but to do justice, and to love kindness, and to walk humbly with your God?' (Micah 6-7-8). 'These are the things which you shall do: speak the truth to one another, render judgments that are true and make for peace . . .' (Zech. 8:16).

This prophetic teaching became somewhat blurred in the writings of the Rabbis, who tended to make no distinction between the commandments of the Bible other than on purely legal grounds. Nevertheless, they too were inclined to see the essence of the Torah in its moral injunctions, such as 'Love your neighbour as yourself' (Lev. 19:18, Sifra 89b). It is also noteworthy that they selected as the Haftarah for the morning of the Day of Atonement the great passage from the book of Isaiah which proclaims that the true fast consists in acts of justice, kindness and compassion (Isa. 58), and that the Confession of Sins (*Viddui*) is an inventory of almost exclusively ethical, not ritual, offences (*Gate of Repentance*, pp. 159-161). In any case, the Rabbis not only included in their Halachah the moral commandments of the Bible, but often elaborated them with exquisite sensitivity, while their corpus of civil law is to a large extent a translation into social policy of the lofty moral exhortations of the Prophets.

But with the Emancipation the civil (*Choshen Mishpat*) part of Rabbinic Law became largely inoperative and even ceased to be studied except by a few, with the result that the ritual law gained undue prominence. This fact, together with others, produced a tendency to equate Jewish practice with ritual observance, and to use such expressions as 'practising', 'observant', *froom* ('pious') and even 'religious' pre-eminently in that narrow sense. So much so that it is commonly considered more 'Jewish' to abstain from pork than to abstain from gossip, and to cover one's head (which, incidentally, Rabbinic Law does not demand at all) than to visit the sick.

This is, of course, a far cry from classical Rabbinic Judaism, and it is even further removed from, indeed it is the antithesis of, Prophetic Judaism. Liberal Judaism has therefore from its inception protested against it as a distortion of the true character of Judaism, and endeavoured to restore a proper perspective and scale of priorities, particularly emphasising the teachings of the Prophets.

In our view, to practise Judaism is first and foremost to obey its moral imperatives in all human relationships: between person and person, husband and wife, parent and child, teacher and pupil, employer and employee, merchant and customer, doctor and patient, judge and litigant, citizen and fellow citizen, ruler and ruled, and so forth. In so far as these relationships are regulated by the laws of the

65

country, it is our duty, as democratic citizens, to influence for good the making and working of these laws, and, as Jews, to do so in the spirit of Judaism and guided by the insights obtainable from the study of our own heritage of Jewish jurisprudence.

13 That you may Remember

The value of observances

The fourth general principle on which we are agreed is the immense importance of Jewish education, since all else depends on it. We therefore see it as our duty to do all we can to intensify it within our Movement, for children and adults alike. This is only partly a matter of the amount of time devoted to it. Much depends also on its quality: that the curriculum should stress what is important; that the modern historical viewpoint should be clearly presented; that the teachers should be well trained, the text-books well written, and the teaching methods up-to-date.

Next, we would stress the communal dimension of Judaism. A Jew who has a sound knowledge of his heritage and conducts his life according to its ethical precepts may seem to have all the qualifications of 'a good Jew'. But he has a further obligation: to help to ensure that the Jewish community remains strong, so that it may be an effective force for good in the life of mankind, and that its religious heritage may be successfully transmitted from generation to generation. This makes it imperative that the individual Jew should help to maintain the institutions of the community, especially its synagogues, and participate as much as possible in their activities. It also means that in all his actions, private and public, he should keep in mind, not only his personal inclinations and predilections, but also the good of *Kelal Yisrael*, of the Jewish Community as a whole. And since the Jews are an international people, this also includes obligations to fellow Jews in other lands, especially those exposed to persecution or insecurity. Within this context, special attention must be given to the State of Israel, chiefly because, as a haven of refuge and in other ways, it serves and benefits the Jewish people as a whole, and partly also because its character and conduct affect profoundly the attitude of the Gentile world to Jews and Judaism.

It should perhaps be added that the concept of *Kelal Yisrael* does not make it necessary, or even desirable, that all Jews should think and act alike. It does mean that no individual or section should unnecessarily infringe the unity of the Community. But 'unnecessarily' means: when no issue of conscience is involved. For important though unity is, integrity is even more important. Besides, unity is not identical with, nor does it depend on, uniformity. On the contrary, since there always has been, is and will be diversity within the Community, which is indeed a sign of health and creativity, its unity depends, rather, on the ungrudging acceptance by all sections of the fact that it is a pluralistic community, and therefore on mutual respect and courtesy in their relations with one another.

Finally, we are convinced of the need for a devotional discipline. This has several aspects. One is study. Though we have already touched on this in the context of religious education, it needs to be added that the regular study of the classical sources of Judaism, by the individual in his own home, in addition to its educational value, also has a devotional value. For it opens his mind and soul to the inspiration of Jewish religious teachings and thereby helps him to attain that consciousness of God, that perceptiveness of spiritual reality, that responsiveness to moral duties and ideals, and that sensitivity towards fellow human beings, all of which are summed up in the word 'holiness'.

Precisely that is, of course, also the purpose of prayer, both private and public. What makes prayer possible is the two-fold fact of God's 'immanence', which we discussed in Chapter 6, and of the 'image of God' in man, which we discussed in Chapter 7. For both reasons, the mind of man, puny though it is, can reach out to, and establish contact with, the infinite Mind of God. When this takes the form of speech, it is called 'prayer'. But it can also be non-vocal and even non-verbal; then it is called 'meditation'. The distinction between the two is not a fundamental one. In either case, what matters is that it should express what the worshipper sincerely thinks and feels towards God. It may be adoration, gratitude, longing, repentance or submission. Accordingly, there are prayers of praise, thanksgiving, supplication, penitence and self-dedication.

Of these, only prayers of supplication (or petition) raise a serious philosophical problem, since they seem to assume that God is sometimes willing to allow Himself to be persuaded by human entreaty to do what He would not otherwise have done. The problem is especially serious when what is requested would involve some interference with the normal operation of the laws of nature, that is, a miracle. Indeed, if what we said about miracles in Chapter 6 is correct, such prayers must be regarded as illegitimate. But even if prayer cannot, in any straightforward sense, influence God, it can certainly influence man. It opens up a channel through which God's power, always available to those who seek it, can flow into the mind of the worshipper. Therefore, if he prays for a spiritual quality (such as, let us say, courage), the effect may very well be an increase of that quality. And since physical health is in many ways affected by the state of mind of the patient (and of those who attend to him), prayers for recovery from illness may also be in many instances justifiable.

In any case, the value of prayer, whatever its nature, lies in the contact with God which it seeks to establish. For such contact elevates the worshipper to a higher level of spiritual consciousness and makes him more responsive to what God demands of him. Prayer, in short, is a form of exercise which serves the purpose of spiritual fitness, just as physical exercise serves the purpose of physical fitness. As such, its importance can hardly be exaggerated.

A further aspect of Judaism's devotional discipline is the practice of what are commonly called rituals, ceremonies or observances. These do not differ essentially from prayers except that, instead of, or in addition to, employing speech, they use other symbols, engaging the senses of sight, sound, smell, movement and the like. They are, one might say, prayers employing visual, auditory, etc., aids. Like study and prayer, they are, as Liberal Judaism has always insisted, only a means to an end. But because of their 'concrete' character, they are especially liable to be loved and performed for their own sake and so to be regarded as if they essentially constituted the 'practice' of Judaism. We therefore reiterate the warning often sounded by our founders, that this is a grave error. To practise Judaism is to lead a good life in the ethical sense. To perform ceremonies (as to study and to pray) only helps us to do that, by inducing the right frame of mind. And even that it can only achieve if the ceremonies are performed in the right spirit, of understanding, sincerity, reverence and joy, and if they are of such a nature as to make it possible and likely that we shall so perform them.

But though the importance of ritual is instrumental and therefore secondary, it is nevertheless considerable. As Dr. Mattuck wrote, 'the value of Jewish ceremonies is that they can help to sanctify life, serve the bond which unites all Jews, and symbolize the historical continuity of Judaism'. Elsewhere he added that 'they have a value for religious education' and that they 'can stimulate devotion to Judaism'. The still further point might be made that rituals are 'gestures of love', expressing devotion to God in something like the way in which a kiss expresses affection between human beings. Above all, and this point is implicit in several of those already made, observances are reminders. They remind us of God, of the spiritual dimension of life, of our moral obligations and ideals, of our duties to our people, and of particular episodes of our history. Some Jewish observances, like the Sabbath, are specifically said to recall the

Creation (*zikkaron l'ma-aseh v'reshit*) and the Exodus from Egypt (*zecher litzi-at mitzrayim*) (see, e.g., *Service of the Heart,* p. 363), others, like the 'fringes' (*Tzitzit*), are intended to remind us, more generally, of our responsibilities as a people with a mission: 'That you may remember and do all My commandments, and be holy unto your God' (Num. 15:14, *Service of the Heart,* p. 33). Only those who never suffer from forgetfulness can dispense with such reminders, and we doubt whether they exist.

For all these reasons we believe that it would be a mistake (which former generations of Liberal Jews were perhaps a little inclined to make) to underestimate the importance of ritual observances in Jewish religious life. Of course, they must be of the right kind. In the ideas they express or imply, they must accord with our honestly held beliefs. In their form, they must be capable of evoking the desired emotional response. In so far as traditional Jewish rituals satisfy these requirements, as very many of them do, so much the better, for then, in addition to all else, they strengthen the sense of 'the bond which unites all Jews' and of 'the historical continuity of Judaism'. In so far as they no longer satisfy these requirements, they must be reinterpreted, modified or given up. And in so far as there may be a need for new rituals, we should be ready to devise them, as we have done in a number of instances.

These, then, are the main principles which guide us in our approach to the practice of Judaism. The details are legion. To describe them fully, tracing their historical origins and traditional interpretations, discussing the reasons for them, and indicating the changes they have undergone in the course of the last 75 years, would require several volumes. But the chapters that follow will, we hope, provide sufficient information within the limited scope of this book.

PART II

THE PRACTICE OF
LIBERAL JUDAISM

1 To Life!

The sanctity of life

When Jews drink a toast, they are likely to say *L'Chayyim*, 'To Life!'. This is no accidental custom; it reflects a zest for life, and a high valuation of life, inculcated by Judaism itself. One of the most dramatic passages of the Bible reads, 'I call heaven and earth to witness against you this day that I have set before you life or death, blessing or curse; therefore choose life, that you and your descendants may live' (Deut. 30:19).

At its deepest level, this reverence for life is rooted in the daring affirmation of the opening chapter of the Bible that God created man in His own image, implying that the 'spirit' or 'soul' of man is God-like and therefore sacred. It follows, too, that the value of human life is infinite and therefore incalculable; it can neither be divided nor multiplied. Hence the great declaration of the Mishnah that 'whoever destroys a single life is considered as if he had destroyed the entire world, and whoever saves a single life as if he had saved the whole world' (San. 4:5).

Accordingly, there is no crime which Judaism abhors more deeply than *shefichut damim*, the shedding of blood, and no virtue which it extols more highly than *pikkuach nefesh*, the saving of life. But Judaism is never satisfied to enunciate general principles; it always seeks to translate them into rules of conduct, both negative and positive. Negatively, it proclaims: 'You shall not murder.' This, the sixth of the Ten Commandments, must not be restricted to the prohibition against taking another person's life without just

75

cause but, as Dr. Hertz commented, 'Jewish ethics enlarges the notion of murder so as to include both the doing of anything by which the health and well-being of a fellow-man is undermined, as well as the omission of any act by which a fellow-man could be saved in peril, distress or despair.'

Positively, Judaism demands that we should go to extreme lengths to save a human life, whether it be our own or that of a fellow human being. Where such a possibility exists, even if the chances are slight, it is not merely permissible but even obligatory to set aside all other commandments, including for instance the observance of the Sabbath and the Day of Atonement, with only three exceptions. These exceptions are idolatry, incest and murder; for, rather than commit any of these, a man, said the Rabbis, should accept martyrdom (Ket. 19a).

There is also a further qualification. Judaism recognizes that it may sometimes be necessary to take life in order to preserve life. For instance, it grants you the right to defend yourself against a would-be murderer and, if necessary, to kill the attacker in self-defence, although Judaism stresses that if you could save yourself by wounding the assailant, rather than by killing him, it is your duty to do so. The difference between murder and self-defence is well illustrated by two classic examples in our ancient literature. In the Talmud we are told how a man came before Rava and said to him, 'A district Governor has ordered me to go and kill so-and-so, otherwise the Governor will kill me'. Rava answered, 'Let him kill you rather than that you should commit murder. Do you think that your blood is redder? Perhaps his blood is redder?' (Pes. 25b).

In the Midrash we find Ben Petura expounding the verse, 'That your brother might live with you'. He refers to two men travelling through a desert and one of them has a flask of water. If he alone drinks the water he will reach town, but if both of them drink they will both die. Ben Petura cites the verse as proving that both should drink and die rather than that one should live while the other dies.

However, Rabbi Akiva says to him, 'that your brother might live with you' means that your life takes precedence over the life of your friend. The difference between Rava's decision and Rabbi Akiva's is that in the former the man would be saving his own life by committing murder, while in the latter it would be an incidental, though tragic, consequence of his duty to save his own life that he could not, at the same time, save the life of his companion. Rabbi Akiva argues that it cannot be right for two lives to be lost if one can be saved. Nor can it be an obligation for one to give the water to the other, because then the recipient would have a similar obligation to give it to the donor! If the donor voluntarily hands over the water because his friend has a wife and children, etc., then, though it might be considered a noble act of self-sacrifice, there is no actual obligation to do it, since it cannot be said to be demanded by the principle of the sanctity of life.

In Judaism suicide is generally condemned because it takes away from God the decision to end a person's life, but Rabbi H. Rabinowicz in *A Guide to Life* (p. 79) sums up the traditional position when he states, 'The Rabbis consider only a premeditated and deliberate act of self-destruction to be suicide; but when there is an act of aberration or sudden impulse, or when there is a doubt, a more lenient view is generally taken and the deceased is given 'the benefit of the doubt'. Liberal Judaism subscribes to this 'more lenient view' and would not discriminate with regard to the burial or mourning procedure for a suicide.

While it is true that the Mosaic law provides for capital punishment for a convicted murderer and for some other crimes, nevertheless the Rabbis made its application almost impossible by hedging it about with strict laws of evidence. In fact, a Law Court (*Sanhedrin*) which imposed one death sentence in seven years or even, according to one view, in seventy years was considered 'oppressive' (Mak. 1:10). It is not surprising that the modern State of Israel has abolished capital punishment except for the crime of genocide.

Capital punishment is no longer regarded by most experts as a uniquely effective deterrent and, therefore, could not be justified as a case of taking life in order to preserve life. The latter principle, however, may well apply to the problem of war which will be considered in Chapter 5.

Judaism shows a certain amount of flexibility with regard to the problems of abortion and euthanasia. While most Jews would object to 'abortion on demand' there is agreement that the child's life should be sacrificed if the mother's life is in danger. This principle can be traced back to the Mishnah (Ohal. 7:6). Most Liberal Jews would be inclined to extend that principle to cover cases where childbirth would be detrimental to the mother's physical or mental health.

Similarly, most Jews would be opposed to active euthanasia but Chief Rabbi Immanuel Jakobovits has stated in *Jewish Medical Ethics* (p. 124) that 'Jewish law sanctions, and perhaps even demands the withdrawal of any factor—whether extraneous to the patient himself or not—which may artificially delay the demise of the final phase'. In other words, under certain conditions one should not actively administer a death blow, but neither should one artificially prolong a dying person's farewell. This can be justified not only from traditional Jewish sources, e.g. Ket. 104a, but also from the words of the outstanding Liberal Jewish Rabbi, Dr. Israel Mattuck, who wrote in *Jewish Ethics* (p. 71), 'When death is inevitable, terrible suffering violates the respect for life'.

2 Love your Neighbour

The Golden Rule

Judaism demands that all human relationships should be guided by the 'Golden Rule' as found in the Book of Leviticus (19:18), 'You shall love your neighbour as yourself'. This was described by Rabbi Akiva as the fundamental principle of the Torah. Hillel presented it in its negative form when a potential convert to Judaism asked for a quick and concise definition of Judaism. Hillel replied, 'What is hateful to you, do not to your fellow-man. That is the essence of the Torah. All the rest is commentary. Go and learn' (Shab. 31a). There are many who would argue that Hillel's formulation is preferable to that of Leviticus since it is more practical. They would assert that it is almost impossible for us to love our neighbour in the same way that we love ourselves, but it is well within the realm of possibility to abstain from actions which might harm him. In fact, the fundamentals of a stable social order are based upon such principles. The law cannot force us to act lovingly toward our neighbour but it can prevent us from doing him any harm.

Moses Maimonides includes among the 613 Commandments (*Taryag Mitzvot*) mentioned in the Torah such negative commandments as not to kill; not to kidnap; not to rob; not to steal; not to oppress; not to deceive; not to defraud; not to humiliate; not to swear falsely; not to testify falsely; not to ignore lost property; not to lead astray; not to gossip; not to hate; not to take vengeance; not to bear any grudge; not to covet; etc., etc. But he also includes many positive commandments such as to imitate God (by being loving, merciful, etc.); to give to the poor; to pay wages promptly; to love strangers; to honour one's parents; to act correctly in business; etc., etc.

We can see that Judaism embraces the teachings both of Leviticus and of Hillel. It combines the ideal goal with the practical steps which can be taken towards it. If God represents the perfection of Love, then the more we learn to love one another the more 'godly' will our life become. Since we recognize the truth in Malachi's words, 'Have we not all one father? Has not one God created us?' (2:10), then it follows that we are all brothers and sisters and that we should love one another accordingly. When we recall the commandment, 'You shall love the stranger, for you were strangers in the land of Egypt' (Deut. 10:19), we realize how much it applies to us in modern times. For instance, if we arrived as refugees in a strange land, with limited financial resources and only a small understanding of the language of that country, would we like to be ostracized, vilified or even ignored? The answer might give us a clue as to how to treat the Pakistanis and other immigrants in our midst.

In assessing how we should act, we need constantly to ask ourselves, 'How would I like others to act towards me if I were in their position?' If I were to be attacked by a gang of youths in the street, would I like passers-by to come to my aid, or would I prefer them to ignore me on the pretext that it is none of their business? If my car were to break down on a lonely road, would I like a passing motorist to stop and enquire whether he can be of assistance or would I like him to go hurtling by? If I were living alone, and were forced by illness to remain in bed, would I like my neighbours to do my shopping, or even to prepare some meals for me, or would I expect them 'to keep themselves to themselves'? If I had lost my job, and did not know where the next week's rent was coming from, would I like an acquaintance to find something for me to do in his business, or would I expect him to say that I must have deserved to be sacked and that I don't deserve to be given another job? The answers to these,

and to many similar questions, give some indication of the meaning and application of 'Love your neighbour as yourself'. There are no civil laws which can compel us to take action in the above instances, but the Jewish religious law tells us that we are obliged to assist those in need of help.

In Chapter 4 we shall consider the many applications of this principle to social and economic justice. Here we would concentrate more upon acts of personal love and kindness. The Rabbis referred to such acts as *Gemilut Chasadim* ('Bestowal of Kindnesses'). They laid special stress on hospitality (*Hachnasat Or'chim*, 'Bringing in Guests'), visiting the sick (*Bikkur Cholim*), comforting the bereaved (*Nichum Avelim*), dowering a (poor or orphaned) bride (*Hachnasat Kallah*) and ransoming prisoners (*Pidyon Shevuyyim*). The Rabbis regarded this form of personal service as being superior to merely giving money to the poor. Nevertheless, the latter is also praised. It is called *Tzedakah* which originally meant 'justice' but later came to mean 'charity' or 'almsgiving' because that was seen as a fulfilment of the obligation to correct injustice. The obligation to give money to the community chest applied even to the poor who were supported by it (Git. 7b).

Maimonides summed up the teaching of the Rabbis by listing eight 'degrees of charity' in descending order of excellence, as follows: (1) To help a poor man to rehabilitate himself and become self-supporting by making him a gift or loan, or entering into a partnership with him, or finding him a job. (2) To give him financial relief in such a way that the donor and recipient are unknown to each other, e.g. by contributing to a community fund. (3) To give in such a way that the giver knows who the recipient is, but the recipient does not know who the donor is. (4) To give in such a way that the recipient knows who the donor is, but the donor does not know the recipient. (5) To give before being asked. (6) To give only when asked. (7) To give less than one should. (8) To give grudgingly.

Finally, we might ask, 'Does Love your Neighbour apply

also to your enemy?' Apart from the special cases of war and crime which are considered in Chapter 5, Judaism answers, 'Yes'. After all, your enemy is also created 'in the image of God' and you must help him as a human being. We find in the Book of Exodus, 'If you meet your enemy's ox or his ass going astray, you shall surely bring it back to him. If you see the ass of one who hates you lying under its burden, and are disinclined to help him, you shall surely help him with it' (23:4ff.). Or, as the Book of Proverbs states, 'If your enemy is hungry, give him bread to eat; and if he is thirsty, give him water to drink' (25:21). Further, a policy of hatred and retaliation is likely to aggravate the situation, so that we are told not to take vengeance or bear any grudge (Lev. 19:18). Instead, we should always work for a reconciliation, 'Forgive your neighbour the wrong he has done, and then your sins will be pardoned when you pray' (Sirach 28:2). No wonder a Rabbi used to pray every night before going to bed, 'Forgiveness to all who have caused me pain' (Meg. 28a), and another said, 'Who is the mightiest among the mighty? . . . He who turns his enemy into a friend' (Avot d'Rabbi Natan 23:1).

3 A Little Sanctuary

The sanctity of family life

Ever since the heathen soothsayer, Balaam, looked at the children of Israel and declared, 'How lovely are your tents, O Jacob, your dwelling places, O Israel' (Num. 24:5), the gentile world has paid tribute to the family life of the Jewish people. The unique role of the family in Jewish life has not arisen through some historic accident but has rather been impressed upon the Jew by design from the earliest times. The second chapter of the Book of Genesis implies a high valuation of the marriage relationship when it declares 'Therefore shall a man leave his father and his mother, and shall cleave unto his wife, and they shall be one flesh' (2:24). Later, the Rabbis were even more emphatic. Rabbi Hanilai, with exaggeration for emphasis, went so far as to say that 'a man who has no wife lives without joy, without blessing and without good' (Yev. 62b), and many others spoke in the same vein. In addition to the companionship which can be enjoyed in marriage, Judaism saw in that institution the opportunity for procreation and the means of establishing a home—a 'little sanctuary'—in which children could be brought up under proper parental guidance.

It is true that according to Biblical and Rabbinic Law men were allowed to marry more than one wife (although women were not allowed to marry more than one husband), yet it is interesting to note that of the hundreds of Rabbis mentioned in the Talmud not one is reported as having more than one wife. Polygamy became increasingly rare and was finally forbidden under pain of excommunication. This decree is traditionally attributed to Rabbi Gershom ben Judah of Mayence, who lived around 1000 C.E., but it has recently been shown to date from the 12th century.

Judaism regulates family life in various ways including the choice of marriage partners. Jewish men and women are urged to look for their marriage partners among their coreligionists. This does not arise from any feeling of 'superiority' over our non-Jewish neighbours. It recognizes that if husband and wife differ in their religious background, affiliation, outlook and practice, they are less likely to achieve the perfect harmony of an ideal marriage. That is why we believe that Hindus should marry Hindus, Moslems should marry Moslems, Roman Catholics should marry Roman Catholics, etc. It should also be noted that a couple which does not share the same religion faces a problem with regard to the religious upbringing of its children which cannot easily be solved—if, indeed, it can be wholly satisfactorily resolved at all. It is also true to state that mixed marriages tend to weaken the Jewish community, since their offspring are less likely to be effectively identified with the community than the offspring of single-religion Jewish marriages.

With regard to the husband/wife relationship, Judaism requires both parties to be faithful to one another and to treat each other with the utmost respect, consideration and affection. A typical saying of the Rabbis is that a man should love his wife as himself and respect her more than himself (Yev. 62b). Rabbinic Law provides detailed instructions as to how each should treat the other, including the 'conjugal rights' of each partner. Judaism regards sexual intercourse as an important aspect of marriage both as a way of expressing unity in love and as a means of procreation. With regard to the latter, the school of Hillel, whose opinion prevailed, considered that a couple had fulfilled their obligation to 'be fruitful and multiply' (Gen. 1:28) when they had produced one son and one daughter (Yev. 6:6).

The problem arose, however, when couples sought

guidance regarding the practice of Birth Control by the use of contraceptive devices. All agree that this is permissible when childbirth could have fatal consequences for the wife. Orthodox Rabbis tend to regard this as the only exception, and to forbid contraception in all other cases mainly as a violation of the prohibition against 'spilling semen to no purpose' (Ned. 20b). The Biblical precedent is Onan's 'sin' (Gen. 38:9). Progressive Judaism permits it more generally, provided that there is no unjustified evasion of the responsibility of parenthood, and that only medically approved methods of contraception are used. As Dr. Martuck wrote in *Jewish Ethics* (p. 120), 'It is a social, and moral duty, that goes with marriage to have children; but it is the duty of parents, constantly emphasized in Judaism, to give children a proper education and general upbringing. That duty can be fulfilled only by considering the economic factors and social conditions which are involved. They justify the regulation of births for the sake of the children'. In fact, the non-Orthodox point of view with regard to Family Planning and Birth Control might be illustrated by statements issued by the two main Rabbinic Groups in the U.S.A. as follows: 'Proper education in contraception and birth control will not destroy, but rather enhance, the spiritual values inherent in the family and will make for the advancement of human happiness and welfare', and 'We urge the recognition of the importance of the control of parenthood as one of the methods of coping with social problems'.

Ideally, Judaism looks on marriage as a life-long union. But it recognizes that when a marriage has broken down irretrievably, and all attempts at reconciliation have failed, the best solution for the individuals concerned may be a divorce, thus enabling them to make a fresh start. Commenting on the passage in Malachi (2:16), 'I hate divorce, says the Lord God, the God of Israel', the Rabbis stated that 'the very altar weeps when a man divorces his first wife' (Git. 90b). And when, alas, a divorce does take place,

Jewish families should rally round the divorced partner and any children involved in order to fill as far as possible the vacuum which has been created.

There are numerous examples in Jewish literature of the obligations placed upon parents with regard to their children, and the obligations of children to their parents. Parents obviously had to provide for their children's physical needs as well as their religious education. The latter was never regarded merely as a duty to send the children to a 'Religion School', but rather should it be undertaken personally by the parents. The injunction, 'And these words which I command you this day shall be upon your heart; and you shall teach them diligently to your children' (Deut. 6:6-7) implies that you can only influence children by personal example. That is why it is important for children to see their parents living up to the moral and ethical standards which they seek to impose upon the family, as well as performing meaningful rituals in the home. While the Rabbis laid the greatest emphasis on the teaching of religion to children, they did not ignore the other necessities of life. 'A father is obligated to teach his son a craft (or a trade) in addition to teaching him Torah. Not to teach him a craft is as though he was preparing him for a career as a thief' (Kid 29a-30a). Similarly the Rabbis compelled a father to provide for his daughter's marriage.

The obligations of children to their parents are also clearly defined in the Bible and the Talmud. The fifth commandment states, 'Honour your father and your mother' (Ex. 20:12, Deut. 5:16), and in the famous 'Holiness' chapter in the Book of Leviticus we find, 'You shall revere every man his mother and his father' (19:3). The Rabbis pointed out that in one of these references 'father' is placed before 'mother' while they are reversed in the second, in order to show that the obligation must be fulfilled equally towards both parents. It is interesting that the Bible specifies 'honour' and 'respect' but does not state 'You shall obey your parents'. The reason is that Judaism permits children to disobey their parents if their parents tell them to do something which is sinful. However, the duty to honour and to respect one's parents covers a large area of life including concern for their physical needs and the avoidance of any act which might cause anguish of mind to them. It is the mutual love and concern between parents and children which lays the foundation for the sanctity of Jewish family life.

In later chapters, specific examples will be given of the manner in which the Sabbath and the Festivals are observed in the home so that the home becomes 'a little sanctuary'. As Dr. Hertz put it in *A Book of Jewish Thoughts* (p. 11), 'The Jew's home has rarely been his "castle". Throughout the ages it has been something far higher—his sanctuary'. In modern times we must ensure that our homes do not become mere boarding houses, or television theatres, but that they retain their sacred nature based upon a loving, compassionate, praying family unit. The Rev. Morris Joseph summed it up in *Judaism as Creed and Life* when he wrote, 'Judaism has ever sought to hallow the home, to make it a shrine at which parents minister to the congregation of the children. Prayer has been the incense, and love the sacrifice. All the chief virtues of the Jewish character have had the home, with its mighty incentives and its hallowed associations, for their nursing-place' (p. 415). No wonder the ancient Prophet Malachi pictured the ideal Messianic Age as being the time when 'the hearts of the parents will be turned to the children and the hearts of the children to the parents' (Mal. 3:24).

4 Justice, Justice

The duty to promote social justice

Nowhere does Judaism show itself more as a down-to-earth religion than in its advocacy of social justice. As Leo Baeck wrote in *Essence of Judaism* (p. 197), 'In Judaism social action is religiousness, and religiousness implies social action'. The Torah demands with particular emphasis, 'Justice, justice, shall you follow' (Deut. 16:20), and constantly urges the children of Israel to show concern for, and to give practical aid to, the widow, the orphan, the poor, the stranger, the oppressed and the distressed. The Hebrew Prophets made an outstanding contribution to civilization as they hammered home the need to relate religious conduct to social justice. Let us quote just a few examples.

Isaiah proclaimed, 'Seek justice, relieve the oppressed, judge the fatherless, plead for the widow' (1:17), and in the third section of Isaiah, the Prophet condemned religious practice which was unrelated to social action: 'Is not this the fast that I have chosen? To loose the fetters of wickedness, to undo the bands of the yoke, to let the oppressed go free, and that you break every yoke? Is it not to deal your bread to the hungry, and that you bring the poor that are cast out to your house? When you see the naked, that you cover him, and that you hide not yourself from your own flesh?' (58:6-7). At the beginning of his prophetic calling, Jeremiah was told that his role would be to sweep away the old corrupt regime and to replace it with something better, 'See I have set you this day over the nations and over the kingdoms to root out and to pull down, to destroy and to overthrow, to build and to plant' (1:10). Later, Jeremiah told the Jews that they would only be restored to their land and to their holy places 'if you thoroughly amend your ways and your doings; if you oppress not the stranger, the fatherless, and the widow, and shed not innocent blood' (7:5-6).

The Prophet Amos proclaimed, 'Let justice well up as waters and righteousness as a mighty stream' (5:24), and he was strong in his condemnation of those corrupt merchants who could not wait to make their unholy gains: 'Hear this, you who would swallow the needy, and destroy the poor of the land saying, "When will the new moon be gone, that we may sell grain? And the Sabbath, that we may set forth corn? Making the ephah small, and the shekel great, and falsifying the deceitful balances; that we may buy the poor for silver, and the needy for a pair of shoes, and sell the refuse of the corn" ' (8:4-6). Similarly, Micah had the unscrupulous land developers in mind when he said, 'Woe to them that devise iniquity and work evil upon their beds! When the morning is light, they execute it, because it is in the power of their hand. They covet fields, and seize them; and houses, and take them away; thus they oppress a man and his house, even a man and his heritage' (2:1-2). He also condemned those who traded in scant measures and false balances, and he summed it all up by saying: 'It has been told you, O man, what is good, and what the Lord does require of you; only to do justly, to love mercy, and to walk humbly with your God' (6:8).

The Rabbinic literature later spelled out in more detail what the Prophets had outlined. On examination it must be admitted that all the benefits of the modern welfare state, all the manifestos of the social activists, all the aspirations of the freedom fighters and the human rights groups can trace their fundamental philosophies to the teachings of the Hebrew Prophets. It is not surprising that these teachings should be the cornerstone of Liberal Judaism which from its inception objected to the way in which ritualistic observance was crowding out the prophetic message with regard to ethical and moral conduct. From the days of the Pittsburgh Platform (1885) of the Central Conference of American Rabbis which declared, 'We deem it our duty to participate in the great task of modern times, to solve, on the basis of justice and righteousness, the problems presented by the contrasts and evils of the present organization of society', down to the current Social Issues Committee of our Union of Liberal and Progressive Synagogues, Liberal Judaism has recognized the indissoluble bond between religion and social justice.

This means that Liberal Jews cannot take a 'neutral' position with regard to the suffering of the poor and the under-nourished. They must strive for a more equitable distribution of the world's resources so that more than half of the world's population does not go to bed hungry every night. This does not mean that Liberal Jews prefer socialism to capitalism or vice versa. Judaism is not committed to any particular economic theory. It cares only about the human relations within a society, demanding that these be characterized by freedom, justice and brotherhood. These conditions may be satisfied by a capitalist society, provided that it is of the 'welfare' kind, or by a socialist society, provided that it safeguards individual liberty. Within these broad limits, the individual Jew is free to use his own judgment as to what kind of economic system is most likely, in the particular circumstances of his country, to produce the ideal society. Or, as Mattuck put it in *Jewish Ethics*, 'Economically a social system must be judged by its capacity to produce wealth; ethically, it must be judged by the human conditions it involves, and by the way the wealth it produces is distributed' (p. 104). Liberal Jews must work for an improved system of industrial relations so that the world is not constantly plagued by strikes and lock-outs, and they must try to create an atmosphere in which the employee does not feel exploited by his employer nor does the employer feel that he is held to ransom by his employees.

Judaism insists that commerce must be conducted honestly and justly, as stated in Leviticus, 'When you sell anything to your neighbour, or buy anything from him, you shall not wrong one another' (25:14), and 'You shall have just balances, just weights, a just ephah and a just hin' (19:36). The same principles would cover the relationship between landlords and tenants. Jews are urged to strive for adequate provision to be made for the aged, the sick, the mentally retarded, and others who suffer from disabilities and are unable to care for themselves. 'You shall not curse the deaf, nor put a stumbling-block before the blind' (Lev. 19:14) refers not only to our concern for the disabled but warns us against taking advantage of our neighbour's limitations. Jews must strive for the protection of law-abiding minorities, and they must combat racial prejudice wherever it manifests itself. When Amos declared, 'Are you not as the children of the Ethiopians unto Me, O children of Israel? says the Lord' (9:7), he was trying to impress upon the people that the black Ethiopians were equally dear in the eyes of God as the Jews. Consequently, no Jew should harbour prejudice against 'blacks' or 'yellows' or 'reds'.

The Bible is also explicit with regard to the relationship between the individual and the State. Jeremiah advised the exiles in Babylon, 'Seek the peace of the city whither I have caused you to be carried away captive, and pray unto the Lord for it; for in the peace thereof shall you have peace' (29:7). Similarly, the Rabbis said, 'Pray for the welfare of the Government, for if men did not fear it they would devour each other' (Mishnah Avot 3:1). Further, a third century Amora, Samuel, laid it down as a general rule that the 'law of the land is law' (Git. 10b). This did not mean that the Jew must 'endorse the establishment' or be completely subservient to the State or to its rulers. When the State or its rulers did wrong, they were to be condemned in the same way as others. For instance, when the mighty King David stole the wife of one of his subjects, the Prophet Nathan did not hesitate to confront him and to condemn him (II Sam. 12). Nor did Elijah condone King Ahab's action when he conspired to take Naboth's vineyard (I Kings 21). In fact, there are exceptional situations in which Jews would be justified in disobeying the Government. As Mattuck put it in *Jewish Ethics* (p. 84), 'Government must be obeyed, except when it issues edicts against the Jewish religion. Loyalty to religion is the supreme duty and must be maintained, even if it entails martyrdom, especially if the fundamentals of Judaism are attacked, such as the belief in the One God, the study of the Law, or vital morality. The authority of governments, and the corresponding duty of individuals to obey them, are limited by the demands of religion. In a conflict between them, religion must prevail'. Rabbi Abba Hillel Silver put it more forcibly when he asserted, 'Tyrants and oppressors must be fought. Insurrection and revolution against tyranny are, under certain conditions, not only justified but mandatory' (*Where Judaism Differed*, p. 240). The lesson for our time applies to the reaction of Jews living in States which carry out policies of oppression with a total disregard for human rights. To be a 'freedom fighter' under such circumstances is to be true both to the prophetic tradition and to Liberal Jewish teaching.

The State must also ensure that justice is administered impartially. 'You shall do no injustice in judgment; you shall not be partial to the poor or defer to the great, but in righteousness shall you judge your neighbour' (Lev. 19:15). This not only refers to the strict impartiality of judge and jury, but it also implies that one should have an equal opportunity to present one's case effectively without consideration of the ability to pay legal fees.

Finally, it must be pointed out that Judaism does not differentiate between the obligations of society and the duties of individuals. One cannot take shelter behind the claim, 'It is none of my business', because Judaism believes that we are all in the same boat, and if anyone bores a hole (albeit under his own seat), it is the concern of all the occupants of that boat. The person who bores a hole in the boat may be guilty of a 'sin of commission', but those who do nothing about it are guilty of a 'sin of omission'. The sins of society and the individual's responsibility must be seen in this context. Reference will be made in the next chapter to the problem of national disarmament and the quest for international peace. Let us conclude this chapter with the words of Abba Hillel Silver, 'Judaism's objectives in the quest of the good society are clearly defined: the end of war, universal peace, international co-operation under the reign of law, the eradication of poverty, the security of the individual against all forms of social oppression, the achievement of unity and freedom among men, the practice of compassion, of cleanness and of sobriety in living—all difficult but not impossible ideals' (*Where Judaism Differed*, p. 157).

5 Seek Peace and Pursue it

The duty to promote international peace

Probably the most frequently used word in the revived Hebrew language is the word *Shalom* which means 'peace'. It is used as a greeting when Jews meet, and it is used as a farewell salutation when Jews part. *Shabbat Shalom*—a peaceful Sabbath—is used every week, and even the *Kaddish* prayer, recited in connection with death, concludes with the words, 'May He who makes peace in His celestial heights grant peace to us, to all Israel, and to all mankind, and let us say, Amen'. The ancient priestly blessing which is still used as a benediction at the conclusion of Liberal Jewish services finishes with the supplication as its climax, 'The Lord lift up His countenance upon you and give you peace!' (Num. 6:26).

Just as peace for the individual is regarded as desirable, so was it recognized that the individual could not enjoy peace unless he was living in a peaceful environment. As mentioned in the previous chapter, Jeremiah gave sound advice to the captives in Babylon when he said: 'Seek the peace of the city whither I have caused you to be carried away captive, and pray unto the Lord for it, for in the peace thereof shall you have peace' (29:7). The Jews have learned from bitter experience that minorities are most vulnerable when conditions of economic instability and political and social strife prevail. That is the reason why the Jews have always been exhorted to become 'peacemakers', as enjoined by the saying of Hillel in the Mishnah: 'Be of the disciples of Aaron, one who loves peace and pursues it' (Avot 1:12). This is a reference to the verse in the Psalms: 'Seek peace and pursue it' (34:15). In fact, the whole scheme of God's unfolding plan for the universe could not be envisaged without 'universal peace' as its consummation. The Hebrew Prophets Micah and Isaiah described the Messianic Age as a period when 'they shall beat their swords into ploughshares and their spears into pruning-hooks; nations shall not lift up sword against nations, neither shall they learn war any more' (Mic. 4:3, Is. 2:4).

Clearly it is the duty of every Liberal Jew to promote international peace. We must remember that the root meaning of the Hebrew word *Shalom* is 'complete' or 'unbroken'. Just as you are not a 'complete' person without peace, so is it impossible for a 'divided' world to enjoy peace. As another Jew, Litvinov, once said at the old League of Nations, 'Peace is indivisible'. That is why there were such high hopes at the founding of the United Nations Organization. It was envisaged as an instrument for settling international disputes and for promoting international peace. It was never anticipated that it would become the platform for gangs of nations to get together to pay off old scores, to barter other peoples' territories in exchange for economic and political privileges, and to replace justice with the majority votes of an ideological caucus. Consequently there are many who despair of the U.N.O. ever becoming an effective instrument for the promotion of international peace. Others, while recognizing its past failures and present limitations, assert that it is the best mechanism currently available to us, and we must persevere in trying to restore it to its original purpose and function.

It is suggested that the International Court should be strengthened; that international legislation should be enacted to outlaw terrorism, hi-jacking and other forms of international gangsterism; that arms-limitation agreements should be more widely promoted; and that the growing gap between the rich nations and the poor nations of the world should be recognized as a contributory factor to instability in the international scene. The rich countries failed to come anywhere near the aid target for the second U.N. Development Decade. They suggested that government aid should equal 0.7 per cent of the Gross National Product, but most developed countries, including our own, contribute less than half of that figure. The type of 'aid' must also be considered anew. Most developing countries do not want straight 'grants' of money. They would prefer technological aid to enable them to develop their own economies, and they would prefer a system of trade which would not involve a rising spiral in the price of imported raw materials linked with controls on the price of their exports. It is also shocking to recognize that the nations of the world spend nearly 7 per cent of all they produce on arms—more than on education, housing or overseas aid.

Despite our earnest quest for peace, the Jew has never accepted the assertion that peace must be obtained 'at any price'. If the price of peace is the surrender of one's religious principles, including the rule of justice and morality, then the Jew would regard war as being preferable to oppression. While we are all appalled at the destruction of life and property which wars bring, Judaism does not subscribe to the 'pacifist' philosophy of life since it regards war as often being the lesser of two evils. When we consider the last world war against the Nazis, we realize that the only option open to the world in 1939 to stop the further expansion of Nazism was to take up arms and to defeat it on the battlefield. Of course one has to consider the difference between 'defensive' as opposed to 'expansionist' wars; whether all other methods of settling the differences between nations have been explored; and whether war and its effects are less evil than that which they seek to abolish. The same principle applies to 'liberation movements'. Judaism would obviously prefer non-violent methods to remedy a wrong, but a strong case can be made for the view that resort to violence is sometimes preferable to collaboration with oppression.

That is why the Maccabean struggle is commemorated in

Jewish history, and that is why the armed struggle against Hitler and the Nazis does not contradict the Messianic quest but rather brings nearer its fulfilment. Peace can only come into the world when evil is destroyed. It is true that many will argue that in a 'nuclear age' we face an entirely different situation. Nobody feared, when war was declared against Germany, that the whole world would be destroyed. But when we realize that a single nuclear submarine now has the fire power of a thousand Hiroshimas, and the nuclear armouries of the super powers can destroy all mankind many times over, we have to admit that even 'righteous wars' might mean the end of civilization. In this context, one can understand the increase in the number of Jewish 'pacifists', and it has even been argued that a civilization which is prepared to use such weapons does not deserve to survive.

Whatever the outcome of any future war might be, it is clearly our duty to work tirelessly to prevent the outbreak of such a war. Whether we work to strengthen the United Nations, or the International Court, or to ban the production of nuclear weapons, or to remove poverty in the less developed countries, it is clear that all of these objectives can only be achieved when the life of individuals and of nations is governed by righteousness, for 'the work of righteousness shall be peace; and the effect of righteousness quietness and confidence for ever' (Isa. 32:17). It is obvious that there can be no peace in the world if we do not have peace in ourselves. Since righteousness (or right conduct) is the goal of our religion, one of the side-effects of our right conduct will be peace at home and abroad. We might conclude this chapter with a prayer taken from a Sabbath Eve service in the Liberal Jewish prayerbook (*Service of the Heart*) as follows: 'Grant us peace, Your most precious gift, O eternal Source of peace, and help us to proclaim its message unto the peoples of the earth. Bless our country, that it may ever be a stronghold of peace, and its advocate in the council of nations. May contentment reign within its borders, health and happiness within its homes. Strengthen the bonds of friendship and

97

fellowship among the inhabitants of all lands, and may the love of Your name hallow every home and heart' (p. 87).

6 You shall not Destroy

The duty to protect the environment

Since God created male and female and said to them, 'Be fruitful and multiply and replenish the earth, and subdue it' (Gen. 1:28), it has been assumed that man had the capacity to control his environment. However, the Club of Rome—to name just one of the many reputable organizations—has shown justifiable concern about the dangerous situation arising from the interactions between industrialization and the depletion of natural resources; between increasing population and food shortage; and between pollution, disease, and rising expectations. Many are concerned that man seems to be losing control of what is going on around him, and the late Albert Schweitzer summed it up when he said, 'Man has lost the capacity to foresee and to forestall. He will end by destroying the earth.' We might recall that God promised Noah that 'the waters shall no more become a flood to destroy the earth' (Gen. 9:15), but that does not prevent man himself from destroying it by pollution, erosion and other environmental hazards.

Robert Arvill, in his *Man and Environment*, states, 'The evidence of environmental contamination is widespread: wild life extinguished, air and soil poisoned, land eroded, waters polluted and other natural resources (coal, oil, metals) wasted. This is not a single major problem but the result of myriad acts of thoughtlessness or ignorance.' He points out how it took millions of years to form the present reserves of oil, gas and coal, and centuries to create the top soil on which life depends, but the pace of our present growth, and

99

the demands which modern industrial life make, threaten to exhaust these resources and to affect our environment in other critical ways unless we take action now. For instance, we have to replace our present careless attitude with a genuine love for the seas and the land, and we must replace the short-term preoccupation with our own times and needs with a responsible attitude regarding what sort of environment we will bequeath to future generations. Judaism teaches that man is God's steward on earth, responsible for all it contains. That is Rashi's comment on the verse in the Psalm, 'The heavens are the heavens of the Lord, but the earth has He given to the children of men' (115:16). A good steward does not fritter away that which is put in his charge.

Foremost among the dangers to our environment is that of pollution. If we define pollution as Arvill does (p. 343), as 'the presence in the environment of substances or forms of energy deriving from man's activities in quantities which have, or may have harmful, offensive and unwanted effects', then we can understand how pollution arises from three major forces. First, there is the problem of population growth. The present world population is expected to have doubled itself by the year 2000, and more than trebled itself in 50 years. Even with our present population the F.A.O. estimates that only 20 per cent of the world population is well fed. Another 40 per cent is fed just adequately for subsistence, while the remaining 40 per cent is starving. If the population of the world is allowed to continue at its present rate, it is not too difficult to foresee not only the problems of widespread hunger which will multiply but also the anti-social effects of over-crowding in many parts of the world. While some countries are going ahead with vigorous 'Family Planning' campaigns, it must be pointed out that of 120 developing countries, only 31 have policies favouring a lower rate of population growth. Another 28 favour family planning for health reasons, while 61 are either indifferent or actively opposed to it! It is interesting to note that Jews all over the world seem to have taken seriously their responsibility in reducing world population growth—too seriously for some! Approximately 82 per cent of the world Jewish population is in three countries—the United States, the U.S.S.R. and Israel. The Jewish reproduction rate in the United States is 8/1,000; in the U.S.S.R. it is 9/1,000; while in Israel it is 16.7/1,000. The world rate for the general population is 30/1,000. It would be difficult to argue that the reduced size of Jewish families is due to a concern for universal conditions of over-crowding in the year 2000. More likely is it due to the aware-ness that a smaller family can be given better opportunities for a comfortable life in modern times, as well as affording a greater degree of 'freedom' to the parents. Those who bemoan the depleted 'numbers' among the Jewish world population should consider the challenge of a more vigorous proselytisation policy. The fundamentalists should also note that the command. 'Be fruitful and multiply', was given at a time when the total world population was two!

Pollution also arises from a technology which is in-adequately based upon ecological precepts, such as re-cycling and works inadequately with and through natural processes. Added to this must be the expectation for material goods which is outstripping the capacity of the earth's resources. We witness the effects of pollution in many ways— on the land, in the air, in the water, and in our wild life. The land can be polluted by chemicals used in agriculture and forestry. Contamination of the soil through the use of pesticides, while achieving a short term advantage, can be harmful to animals and plants, including man himself. The fertility of certain species of predatory birds has suffered, and their numbers have been drastically reduced, through pesticides. Pollution of the land also occurs through the by-products of industrial processes and by solid wastes from urban settlements, farms and industry. Soil erosion has been another serious blot upon man's record in dealing with the land. In an endeavour to extract the maximum product as quickly as possible, man has indulged in over-cultivation, deforestation, over-grazing and a general attitude of 'taking out' from the soil without putting anything back. We might recall the 'Eleventh Commandment' broadcast over Jerusalem radio in 1939 by Dr. Walter D. Lowdermilk, 'Thou shalt inherit the holy earth as a faithful steward conserving its resources and productivity from generation to generation. Thou shalt safeguard thy fields from soil erosion, thy living waters from drying up, thy forests from desolation, and protect thy hills from overgrazing by the herds, that thy descendants may have abundance forever. If any shall fail in this stewardship of the land, thy fruitful fields shall become sterile, stony ground, or wasting gullies, and thy descendants shall decrease and live in poverty or perish from off the face of the earth.'

It is a tribute to the modern State of Israel that she has set a wonderful example to the world in land reclamation and in combatting soil erosion. No doubt she is acting in the spirit of the Bible which advocated a 'year of release' when all land was to lie fallow (Lev. 25:4) and which insisted upon the preservation of trees even in wartime (Deut. 20:19). This law, known as *Bal Tash-chit* (You shall not destroy), was later given an even wider interpretation as a prohibition against any wanton destruction, and might well serve as the motto of modern environmentalists.

Our polluted air contains particles of rubber from tyres and asbestos from brake linings. Smoke stacks and exhaust pipes pour forth carbon monoxide, sulphur dioxide and various oxides of nitrogen. These chemicals can affect our health, and in the case of sulphur and nitrogen oxides they are capable of corroding metals and concrete. The individual draws 26,000 breaths daily, most of which—if not all—are of polluted air! No wonder the lungs of town people are usually grey in colour, while those of country people are pale pink. Nor have we yet considered the effect of radioactivity caused by nuclear fall-out, etc.

The increasing pollution of our rivers and streams linked with the increased demand for water for private and industrial purposes indicates the seriousness of the problem.

Many rivers—including the Rhine—have been described as 'open sewers'. The filth and refuse from towns and industries pour into the rivers and poison the aquatic flora and fauna. Add to this the chemicals and pesticides from farms and forests, and the increasing menace of oil pollution, and we can understand why many are concerned about water pollution. It is often stated that man can live without bread but he cannot live without water.

The threat to wild life is also posed by the consumption of chemical substances which are poisonous and which are sprayed indiscriminately upon fields and trees, as well as the destruction of their habitats. The World Wildlife Fund shows that approximately 280 mammals, 350 birds, 80 reptiles, 80 freshwater fish and 30 amphibians are in danger of extinction and can only survive if man desists from some of his activities which now threaten them.

It is worth noting here the emphasis which Judaism places upon kindness to animals. The Bible legislates that one may not take the mother-bird away from her young (Deut. 22:6-7), plough with an ox and an ass yoked together (Deut. 22:10), or muzzle an ox when threshing the corn (Deut. 25:4). The Fourth Commandment states that animals, as well as human beings, must rest on the Sabbath (Ex. 20:10, Deut. 5:14), and the Book of Proverbs states, 'A righteous man has regard for the soul of his beast' (12:10). The first-century Jewish historian Josephus tells us that Jews generally stayed away from the Roman circuses because they involved cruelty to animals. The Rabbis enacted further laws for the protection of animals, for instance that it is forbidden to acquire a domestic animal if one is unable to feed it properly (Pal. Tal. Yev. 14d), that one should always feed one's animal before sitting down to one's own meal (Ber. 40a), and that one may break the Sabbath to relieve animals of pain or danger (Shab. 128b). It is significant that a Jew, Louis Gompertz, was the first to plead for legislation to protect animals in England (in a book entitled *Moral Inquiries on the Situation of Man and Brutes*, published in 1824) and he helped to found the Society for the Prevention of Cruelty to Animals, which he served as Hon. Secretary for many years. While Judaism forbids the infliction of unnecessary suffering on animals (*Tza-ar Ba-aley Chayyim*), it does not forbid the killing of animals for food, provided that it is done as painlessly as possible. To that end it developed a particular method of slaughter about which we shall have more to say in another chapter.

In summing up, we may ask what can the Liberal Jew do about the protection of our environment? First, we must be sure that our information is correct. The average layman is in no position to judge whether this detergent is less liable to cause pollution than that one, or whether the use of aerosols will affect the upper ozones of the atmosphere. Nor does he know whether the dangers created by the population explosion can be countered by Zero Population Growth or whether it is merely a matter of increased food production from sources yet untapped. He does not know whether the development of nuclear energy, as an alternative to the use of oil, is a real threat to the environment apart from being costly in its development. He does not know whether the 7 per cent of all they produce, which the nations of the world spend on arms, could be productively diverted to environmental projects. But he should know that there are a number of bodies working on the international level in order to bring about world-wide concerted efforts in such areas as population control, the protection of land, water and air from pollution, increased food production and better distribution, the abolition of slums, the protection of wild-life, the seeding of hurricanes, cheaper methods of desalination and so on.

As Liberal Jews, we must press our Government to support these organizations even if it occasionally means the sacrifice of some temporary national gain. Similarly, within our nation, we must ensure that adequate funds are available for scientific research into problems relating to the environment, and we must be prepared to sacrifice certain aspects of our personal liberty in order to ensure that the interests of society and of future generations are safeguarded. It must be the responsibility of industry to prove that any new product will not be harmful to the environment before it is unleashed upon the general market, and land developers must continue to be monitored by careful town and country planning legislation. In our personal life, we must take care how we dispose of our litter, when and where we fish, and when we should shoot birds, what size families we produce, what sort of petrol we use, whether the noise from our radio or hi-fi system is polluting our neighbourhood, etc. The Jew has always been prepared to make sacrifices for his children. As citizens, we must be prepared to make similar sacrifices to ensure that future generations will be able to enjoy a healthy and pleasant existence.

7 To Learn and to Teach

The need for religious education

The importance of 'learning' is derived from such scriptural references as, 'Hear, O Israel, the statutes and ordinances which I speak in your ears this day, that you may learn them, and observe them faithfully' (Deut. 5:1), and 'This book of the Torah shall not depart out of your mouth, but you shall meditate on it day and night, that you may faithfully observe all that is written in it' (Josh. 1:8). The importance of 'teaching' is derived from such verses as, 'And these words which I command you this day, shall be upon your heart; and you shall teach them diligently to your children' (Deut. 6:6-7). In Judaism, this *Mitzvah* (commandment, duty)—to learn and to teach—is called *Talmud Torah*. Unfortunately, the majority of the Rabbis of the Talmudic period took the view that this twofold duty applied only to males, so that Jewish mothers were not required to teach their children, and Jewish daughters did not have to be taught, with the result that for many centuries Jewish women tended to be uneducated. However, Progressive Judaism, from its inception, rectified this inequality by providing religious instruction for boys and girls alike, and in this respect its example has now been followed by most branches of Orthodox Judaism.

It should be noted, from the quotation cited above, that one cannot teach children diligently unless God's words are first on the hearts of the parents. This implies learning and practising before one is effectively able to teach. There are many who advocate a sort of 'Juvenile Judaism' (saying, 'we must ensure that our children are taught about their religion'), while there are a few who recognize the prior need for an 'Adult Judaism' (saying, 'we must ensure that we know and practise our religion before we can expect our children to follow our example'). Judaism believes that religious education will never be effective until those who teach are prepared to set an example themselves.

The purpose of religious education in general is to equip the individual to understand his role in life and to develop a sense of values which will show him how to live. Jewish religious education would obviously give guidance according to Jewish teaching and tradition. It will also assist the individual to understand why he is 'different' as a Jew or, as Leo Baeck put it in *The Essence of Judaism* (p. 267), 'All education had to aim at this preservation, the preservation of men for the sake of their special peculiarity and their special spiritual possessions, so that they might live not merely for the sake of living, but for the sake of living in Judaism'. To appreciate his Jewish heritage it would be necessary for the Jew to become familiar with Jewish history, Jewish culture, the Hebrew language, Jewish thought and practice. He would have to become aware of his link with God, his place in the Jewish community, and his obligation to the world at large. Clearly this would involve a programme of study which should begin as early as possible but could hardly be expected to terminate at Bar-Mitzvah or Confirmation. Nevertheless, a good foundation is important. That is why the Book of Proverbs declares, 'Train up a child in the way he should go, and even when he is old he will not depart from it' (22:6).

Judaism regards the home as the first and major training-ground of Jewish religious education. From its earliest impressions, the child should absorb the spirit and practices of Judaism in its experience in the home. It will grow up seeing the candles kindled on the eve of the Sabbath and of Festivals; it will take an increasing part in the home *Seder* and in the kindling of the candles in the *Chanukkiyyah*; it will hear the *Kiddush* being recited and will learn the responses in the Grace; it will learn to say its night and morning prayers; it will witness the hospitality extended to visitors, and will participate in the circle of love which binds the family together; and the home will also help it to share the joys and the sorrows which inevitably descend upon us all. Even before it attends formal religion classes, the child should be introduced to books of Jewish interest in the home. It should quickly be made aware of the fact that it belongs to the 'people of the Book'. As H. G. Wells stated in his *Outlines of History* (p. 235), 'The Jewish religion, because it was a literature-sustained religion, led to the first efforts to provide elementary education for all the children in the community'. No doubt he was aware of the contribution made by the Pharisees which led to the introduction of universal education in Palestine in the first century B.C.E.— about 2,000 years earlier than in most Gentile societies. The Talmud records how Rabbi Joshua ben Gamla ordered that teachers should be appointed in every district and in every city and that boys should be sent to them at the age of six or seven years (Baba Batra 21a).

Almost as important as the home was the school. According to Jewish law a synagogue may be converted into a school, but a school may not be converted into a synagogue. In our own time, the religion school should be given equal consideration and respect. Attending the religion school, the child should find there at least as good conditions for study as it would obtain at its secular school. There should be suitable accommodation equipped with modern furniture and materials. Specially trained teachers should be familiar with all the techniques of audio-visual aids, project-teaching, graduated text books, remedial reading, etc. While it may not be of much value to expect the pupils to recite lists of the Kings of Israel and Judah, it would be beneficial, for instance, to use the Hebrew Prophets for considering guidance for personal conduct, national problems, social justice, reward and punishment, messianism and universalism, the Jewish mission, etc. Most important of all, the teachers must know that religion is 'caught not taught', and that their greatest influence will come from the example which they themselves set.

Clearly there must be a link between the home and the religion school, and an active Parent-Teacher Association can do much to complement the activities of both parents and teachers. Most Jewish children—with the exception of those who attend Jewish Day schools—find themselves as a small 'minority' in their secular schools, and they may well nurse some sort of resentment, or inferiority complex, if an antidote is not provided. It is important, therefore, that at least once a week they attend a school where they know that all the other children share their beliefs, and where they can learn the positive value of those distinctive beliefs. They should also be able to focus their minds upon the Synagogue as their community home and upon its members as their spiritual brothers and sisters. Where Jewish observance in the home is limited for some reason, it is important for the children from that home to avail themselves of residential holiday schools and camps where they can experience an extended period of living in a Jewish atmosphere.

The importance of a good religious education for children is obvious, but we must not overlook the need to build upon that foundation. Judaism has always regarded adult education as being so vital that our great heroes have been the 'scholars' rather than the generals or the business tycoons. In fact, it is only with the maturity that comes with adulthood that one can appreciate to the full the value of the Jewish heritage. Such concepts as the unity of God, the Messianic goal, the need for social justice, particularism and universalism, the role of *Mitzvot*, and the meaning of spiritual immortality are not comprehensible to the juvenile mind. It is only as adults that we can begin to give them serious consideration, and they are an essential part of Jewish religious education. It is right, too, that we should study the thought and practice of religions other than our own, but unless we are reasonably grounded in our own heritage, we are hardly likely to be in a position to make comparisons. Similarly, it is important for Progressive Jews to know as much as possible about other forms of Judaism for, in addition to the intrinsic importance of such knowledge, it is necessary for a proper understanding of the changes which Progressive Judaism has made.

Before the persecution of Eastern European Jewry in the last century, adult Jewish education was widespread. As the pogroms forced many of them to emigrate to this country, their children were taught that, as Jews, they should strive to become good Englishmen. They succeeded but, alas, adult Jewish education declined. Now it is our task to teach their grandchildren that, as good Englishmen, they should strive to become good Jews. Adult education is the only answer. As Mordechai Kaplan put it, 'Where Jewish education is neglected, the whole content of Judaism is reduced merely to an awareness of anti-Semitism. Judaism ceases then to be a civilization, and becomes a complex'.

8 The Service of the Heart

The importance of prayer

The obligation to pray was derived by the Rabbis from the injunction, 'You shall serve the Lord your God' (Ex. 23:25), taken in conjunction with the phrase, 'To love the Lord your God, and to serve Him with all your heart' (Deut. 11:13). 'What,' asked the Rabbis, 'is this service of the heart?' And they answered: 'You must say it is prayer' (Ta'anit 2a).

The Jewish religion has a prayer for almost every conceivable occasion, from the time one opens one's eyes in the morning until the time one closes one's eyes at night. Some examples of these various Blessings (*Berachot*) are as follows:

Grace before meals (or before eating bread).
We praise You, O Lord our God, King of the universe, who bring forth bread from the earth.

Before eating any food, other than bread, made out of wheat, barley, etc. (e.g. cake and biscuits).
We praise You, O Lord our God, King of the universe, who create various kinds of food.

Before eating any other kind of food (e.g. meat, fish, eggs or cheese).
We praise You, O Lord our God, King of the universe, by whose word all things exist.

On hearing thunder.
We praise You, O Lord our God, King of the universe, whose strength and might fill the world.

On hearing good news.

We praise You, O Lord our God, King of the universe, who are good and who do good.

On hearing of a death.

We praise You, O Lord our God, King of the universe, who are the true Judge.

On the positive side, the learning of these Blessings encourage an automatic response to events by the individual which links him with God. On the negative side, there is the danger that the words may come from the lips without registering upon the mind and heart. Consequently, some would advocate that a spontaneous prayer would be preferable. While Liberal Judaism encourages the latter, it also recognizes that many people need the discipline and the training of 'set' prayers before they are able to respond in their own individual way.

Orthodox Judaism demands that men over the age of 13 years should put on phylacteries (*Tefillin*) every morning, except on Sabbaths and Festivals, prior to reciting the Morning service (*Shacharit*). The *Tefillin* are a pair of leather boxes, with straps attached, containing strips of parchment on which are inscribed four passages from the Pentateuch. Each of these passages includes the phrase 'You shall bind them for a sign upon your hand, and they shall be for frontlets between your eyes'. In all probability, this phrase was meant metaphorically as an injunction that 'they'—meaning the words of the Torah in general—were never to be far from the Jew's mind. But the Pharisees interpreted the phrase literally and took 'they' to refer to the particular passages, as above, in which it occurs; so they devised the *Tefillin*. One of the boxes is tied to the left forearm, opposite the heart, and its strap is wound round the arm down to the fingers; the other box is tied to the forehead, with its straps hanging down over the front of the shoulders. While Liberal Jews appreciate the motive behind this custom—as an outward aid to inner piety—they have not generally found its form appealing, particularly if it leads to an over-emphasis upon 'externals' in prayer, and Liberal Judaism does not therefore urge its observance. It does, however, encourage individuals and families to pray every morning and every evening, and the *Service of the Heart* prayerbook provides samples of such daily services (pp 29-56).

The word for prayer in Hebrew is *Tefillah*. The exact origin of the word is not certain; there are various theories about it. But one thing is clear; it does not mean 'petition', as the word 'prayer' does in English. We must, therefore, keep in mind that Jewish prayer is not necessarily of the petitionary kind; as Claude Montefiore wrote in *Liberal Judaism* (p. 51), 'To pray is not the same as to pray for'. Nor is prayer a method whereby we order God to conform to our wishes, least of all to perform 'miracles' by altering His laws of Nature, or suspending their operation, and so disrupting the normal chains of cause-and-effect. In prayer we seek to understand what God would have us do rather than tell Him what He should do. It should not encourage us to look for selfish gain but rather should it teach us to be prepared for unselfish sacrifice. Much of Jewish prayer is in the nature of praise and thanksgiving. God does not need our praise, but we need to praise and to thank Him. As an American Reform Rabbi, Emil G. Hirsch, wrote, 'True worship is not a petition to God: it is a sermon to our own selves'. Reference is made in other chapters to the special prayers which should be recited in the home on Sabbaths and Festivals and on other special occasions.

Mention might be made here of the Jewish custom of covering the head in prayer. Indeed, some Orthodox Jews make a point of keeping their heads covered at all times, generally using for that purpose a skull-cap called *Kippah* (Hebrew), *Kappel* (Yiddish) or *Yarmulka* (a Slav word). We should note that (a) this custom is not mentioned in the Bible (b) it is nowhere required in the entire halachic literature, from the *Mishnah* to the *Shulchan Aruch* (c) the Jews of Palestine and Europe worshipped bareheaded from remotest antiquity until the late Middle Ages. The contrary custom of covering the head, especially when praying, apparently originated in Babylonia where it conformed with prevailing etiquette as an expression of respect, and gradually spread throughout the Islamic world, including Palestine and Spain, before penetrating into Christian Europe. While most Jews are now so accustomed to this practice as to take it for granted, some prefer to worship bareheaded, as their remote ancestors did, on the ground that this is the modern way of expressing respect, at least in the Western world. This variety of choice is reflected in Liberal Jewish congregations.

More securely grounded in Jewish tradition is the prayer-shawl (*Tallit*). This is derived from a law in the Pentateuch requiring the Israelites to 'Make themselves fringes (*Tzitzit*) on the corners of their garments' (Num. 15:38-39) as a reminder of their religious obligations. It is worn by male Jews during the morning service (in the synagogue or at home) and during all services on the Day of Atonement. Additionally, it is worn as a 'vestment' by the clergy and by any lay people who take an active part in the leadership of the service (e.g. when opening the Ark, or when being called to the Scroll). In a few Progressive synagogues around the world women have begun to assert their 'equality' by donning the *Tallit*. Some Jews wear a smaller version of the Tallit, known as *Tallit Katàn* (Small *Tallit*) or *Arba Kanfot* (Four Corners) under their outer garment at all times.

Finally, a word about communal worship. One often hears the absentee worshipper asserting 'I don't need to go to the synagogue. I can pray just as well at home!' Such statements usually indicate a complete ignorance of the differing purposes of personal and communal worship. One is not an alternative to the other—both are necessary. In personal prayer, one gives expression to individual aspirations and sentiments. In communal worship, we recognize that we are part of a greater whole and that we have common obligations and aspirations which we share with our co-religionists. It creates a greater sense of our interdependence under God.

Regular services in the synagogue establish set times during the week when many people will be certain to think about God and their responsibilities to Him. They will help to 'rouse and stimulate the activity of the spirit in the individual'. In addition, many people find it easier to pray in a house of worship because the physical and human environment are often more conducive to prayer. One's physical presence, too, contributes to the 'group spirit' which often assists some other worshipper who has come to a service seeking comfort, consolation or elevation of spirit. It must also be noted that public worship in Judaism is not only a matter of prayer but also of study. The Jewish liturgy is interspersed with passages from Jewish literature which have an educational purpose, and the scriptural readings and the sermon should serve the same purpose. That is why the Rabbis, though they attached great importance to private prayer, urged Jews to 'pray with the congregation' whenever possible.

9 The House of the Lord

The role of the Synagogue

'I rejoiced when they said unto me: "Let us go to the house of the Lord"' (Psalm 122:1). Such verses abound in the Book of Psalms. They refer to the Temple in Jerusalem where the Israelites worshipped for many centuries. Then the services were conducted by priests, who owed their privilege to their alleged descent from Aaron, and consisted chiefly of animal and other sacrifices, while the lay people looked on. But when the Temple was finally destroyed (by the Romans) in 70 C.E., another institution—the Synagogue—stood ready to take its place. Some believe that it originated during the Babylonian exile in the 6th century B.C.E., others associate its emergence with the rise of the Pharisees in the 2nd century B.C.E. Nobody doubts that there were already many synagogues, both in Palestine and in the Diaspora, in the 1st century B.C.E.

The word synagogue is Greek for 'assembly' and a translation of the Hebrew *Beyt ha-Kneset* (House of Assembly). As this term implies, it is essentially a 'democratic' institution, for in the synagogue congregational prayer and study took the place of the sacrificial cult of the Temple. Since this did not require priests, lay people were enabled and encouraged to participate actively, even to lead the service in so far as they possessed the necessary knowledge. For over 2,000 years, therefore, the Synagogue has been the chief institution of the Jewish people. It has been for them what the Temple was previously: 'The House of the Lord'.

Synagogues have been built in many different architectural

styles, depending upon local fashion and the community's means. In the Middle Ages it was considered desirable that the synagogue should tower above all surrounding buildings, but that is not often feasible and no longer demanded. Even an ordinary house or room can be turned into a synagogue; it acquires its 'sanctity' by being so designated and used.

The most sacred object in a synagogue is the 'Scroll of the Law' (*Sefer Torah*). This contains the Hebrew text (without vowels) of the Pentateuch, hand-written by a qualified Scribe (*Sofer*) on strips of parchment which are sewn together and attached to wooden rollers. It is wrapped in an embroidered mantle and adorned with silver ornaments. The latter traditionally include a pair of crowns (sometimes called *Rimmonim*, 'Pomegranates'), a 'breast-plate' (*Choshen*) reminiscent of that worn by the High Priest in ancient times, and a 'pointer' called *Yad* (hand) which is used by the reader in order not to touch the Scroll with his finger.

A synagogue usually has several Scrolls, so that on certain occasions different passages may be read from different Scrolls. They are kept in a structure of wood or other materials which is generally called *Aron ha-Kodesh* (the Holy Ark). Traditionally, the congregation is supposed to face towards Jerusalem during the more solemn prayers. To facilitate this, the Ark, in Western countries, is normally sited on the east wall. In front of the Ark there is a 'Perpetual Light' (*Ner Tamid*), a reminder of one in the Temple (Ex. 27:20), and a symbol of the Presence of God and of the spiritual light that emanates from the Torah. The service is conducted from a raised platform known as the *Bimah* (a Hebrew word) or the *Almemar* (an Arabic word). This may be either in the centre of the synagogue or immediately in front of the Ark.

Traditionally, a full congregational service requires the presence of a *Minyan* (Quorum) consisting of at least 10 men aged 13 years or over. Progressive synagogues do not generally regard this as essential and, in any case, they would not exclude women. The Talmud states, 'All are qualified to be among the seven (who are called up to read the Torah), even a minor and a woman, only the sages said that a woman should not read the Torah out of respect for the congregation' (Meg. 23a). However, Rashi's comment on this passage implies that it was not uncommon for women to read the Prophetic lesson. It is therefore likely that in the ancient synagogues men and women sat together. However, during the Middle Ages the exclusion of women from education combined with social etiquette to bring about the segregation of the sexes in the synagogue. This is still the rule in Orthodox synagogues, while Progressive synagogues have reverted to mixed seating.

According to Jewish Law, the prayers may be recited in any language. Not only the Mishnah (Sotah 7:1) but all the Codes make it clear that all prayers (with the sole exception of the Priestly Benediction) may be recited in the vernacular, and in ancient times this permissiveness was used. Some ancient prayers were actually written in Aramaic, the vernacular of the time, and in the period of the Mishnah every synagogue had an interpreter (*Meturgeman*) who orally translated the Scripture portions into the vernacular. Later, however, that practice ceased and, apart from a few Aramaic prayers, Hebrew became the exclusive language of Jewish public worship. That is still the practice in Orthodox Judaism. Progressive Judaism, however, has re-introduced the use of the vernacular, even while retaining the use of Hebrew to an appreciable extent. We include Hebrew because we recognize that it is the historic language of the Jewish people. Most of our sacred literature as well as our classical liturgy was written in that language and no translation can convey adequately its full meaning and nuances. We also recognize that Hebrew can form a common international link with other Jews so that we can form a bond of solidarity with them in our communal worship. On the other hand we regretfully recognize that not all Jews can read or can understand the Hebrew language as well as they should. Therefore, there is the danger of the service—if it is conducted entirely in Hebrew—becoming entirely or largely incomprehensible to a substantial proportion of worshippers, thus defeating the very purpose of worship.

In most Liberal synagogues the *Sefardi* pronunciation of the Hebrew is used. It is the same pronunciation as is used in modern Israel. Most of the Orthodox service is chanted by the *Chazzan* (Cantor), with the rest of the congregation joining in at various stages. In Liberal synagogues, most of the service is read by the Rabbi or a Lay Reader, sometimes alone, sometimes in unison or responsively with the congregation. While Orthodox choirs are generally all-male, and there is no instrumental music (except on such occasions as weddings), in Liberal synagogues there are mixed choirs which are organ-accompanied. Some Liberal synagogues also employ a Cantor.

The Jewish liturgy has a long history. Essentially, it is a creation of the Pharisees; therefore the oldest prayers date from pre-Christian times. However, every subsequent age made its additions. For many centuries this ever-growing material was handed down orally. The first Jewish prayer-book as such was written by Amram Gaon in the 9th century. After that, especially after the invention of printing in the 15th century, prayerbooks were published in ever larger numbers. A prayerbook for weekdays and Sabbaths is generally called a *Siddur* (arrangement), and a prayerbook for the Festivals is called a *Machzor* (Cycle).

All traditional Jewish prayerbooks are essentially similar, though there are minor variations, especially between *Sefardi* (Spanish) and *Ashkenazi* (German) ones. Liberal Judaism, however, has revised the traditional liturgy fairly extensively. In particular, it has omitted many of the *Piyyutim* (medieval poems), reduced the amount of repetition, generally shortened the services, and eliminated or re-written those prayers which it regarded as antiquated in doctrine (e.g. references to a personal Messiah, the ingathering of the exiles, the rebuilding of the Temple, the restoration of animal sacrifices and the physical resurrection of the dead). In addition, it has selected from classical Jewish sources many passages which do not feature in the traditional liturgy, and composed many new prayers and meditations expressing contemporary thoughts, moods and aspirations.

Each of the services in a synagogue consists principally of a series of benedictions (*Berachot*) known collectively as the *Tefillah* (Prayer) or, because they are traditionally recited standing, as the *Amidah* (Standing). Yet another name for the series is *Shemoneh Esreh* (18), because that is the number of benedictions it contained in the days of the *Mishnah;* later a nineteenth was added. On weekdays, all nineteen are recited; on Sabbaths and Festivals, only the first three and the last three, the intermediate ones being replaced by one relating to the Sabbath or Festival in question (three on New Year). The Morning and Evening services also include the recitation of the *Shema*, beginning *Shema Yisrael, Adonai Eloheynu, Adonai Echad* (Hear, O Israel, the Lord is our God, the Lord is One). The *Shema* is preceded and followed by other benedictions.

The reading of the Torah takes place mainly on Sabbath and Festival mornings, and on the afternoon of the Day of Atonement, but traditionally also on Monday and Thursday mornings (which used to be assize days and market days, so that the villagers would gather in the towns) and Sabbath afternoons. For this purpose, the Torah is divided into weekly portions, each being known as the *Parashah* or *Sidrah* of the week, so that the whole Torah is completed in one year. Traditionally, a number of congregants are 'called up' to participate; the privilege of doing so is called an *Aliyah* (going up). One takes out the Scroll, a task known as *Hagbahah* (lifting up); one undresses the Scroll, a task called *Gelilah* (rolling); several more (seven on Sabbath morning, fewer on other occasions) share the reading or just recite the benedictions before and after each sub-section of the Scroll reading. On Sabbath and Festival mornings, and on the afternoon of the Day of Atonement, the reading of the Torah is followed by a reading from the Prophets which is called *Haftarah* (Dismissal), the person who reads it being known as the *Maftir*. In Liberal Synagogues, the general custom is to read only an extract from the weekly portion of the Torah, but then to translate it into the vernacular, and to read the *Haftarah* in the vernacular only. Hence the number of persons 'called up' is generally reduced to the Ark openers (i.e. those who perform *Hagbahah* and *Gelilah*), one who recites the benedictions before and after the Scroll reading, and the *Maftir*.

To conclude the service there are a number of prayers and hymns. One concluding prayer is the *Aleynu* (It is our duty.); another is the *Kaddish* (Holy) which is mainly in Aramaic. Both of these prayers express a fervent longing for the coming of the Messianic Age. The *Kaddish* is also a mourner's prayer. Of the concluding hymns, the best known is the *Adon Olam* (Eternal Lord)—probably dating from the 11th or 12th century—which epitomizes the Jewish conception of God.

The synagogue is usually described as serving a three-fold purpose. It is a House of Prayer (*Beyt Tefillah*), a House of Study (*Beyt ha-Midrash*) and a House of Assembly (*Beyt ha-Kneset*). We have already described the synagogue in its role as a House of Prayer. Now we must consider its other purposes.

Since the inception of the Synagogue, it has served as a centre of study for the Jewish community. That is why the Jewish people was literate at a time when most of the remainder of the world was steeped in ignorance. In its tender years, the Jewish child would be taken to the synagogue where it would be introduced to the Hebrew language and where it would begin to study the sacred literature. This process continues to this day. A Religion School (*Cheder* or *Talmud Torah*) is held at least once a week (usually on a Sunday morning), and some synagogues also hold midweek evening classes where the children study the Jewish religion, the Bible, post-Biblical Jewish literature, Jewish history, the Hebrew language, etc. The synagogue is also used as a centre of adult Jewish education, and many synagogues contain a Jewish library.

The third aspect of activity within a synagogue is its use as a House of Assembly. As a minority throughout the Diaspora it has been necessary for the Jewish community to have some central meeting place where its members could meet for social, cultural and charitable activities. Consequently the synagogue premises often include facilities for Youth group activities, Ladies' Guilds, Friendship Clubs for pensioners, Zionist societies and other charitable and cultural activities. Nor should it be forgotten that the Rabbi's office is usually housed in the synagogue building, acting as a clinic for the numerous spiritual problems which are brought there.

10 Observe the Sabbath Day

The value of the Sabbath

The 'special' days in the Jewish year, like the special days in our secular life, are marked by a number of observances. Such a day is the *Shabbat* (Sabbath), from a Hebrew word meaning 'to rest'. We all look forward to our annual holiday, counting the months, weeks and days which will bring us to the time when we can get away from our regular routine, enjoy a complete change and rest, and become refreshed and re-invigorated ready to face another year. Judaism believes that we can enjoy this 'holiday' weekly instead of annually, and the name that it has given to this 'holy day' is the Sabbath.

The Bible refers to its institution in the context of the act of Creation and as one of the Ten Commandments. The latter emphasizes that the Sabbath is a great social institution, giving all citizens, and even animals, periodic respite from work. This was especially important for slaves, for it gave them a taste of freedom, and the dignity of freedom. Accordingly the Sabbath came to be regarded as 'a memorial of the Exodus from Egypt'—a reminder of the Israelites' own liberation from slavery. In addition to its great social benefit the Sabbath also has a spiritual purpose. The leisure it provides is to be used positively, for the cultivation of the higher side of human nature: for meditation, prayer, worship, study and family 'togetherness'.

In the Exodus version of the Decalogue, the Fourth Commandment begins, 'Remember the Sabbath Day, to sanctify it'. In the Deuteronomy version it begins 'Observe the Sabbath Day, to sanctify it'. The Rabbis understood the former to allude to the positive observance of the Sabbath by means of ceremonies such as *Kiddush* (see below), and the latter as an allusion to its negative observance, i.e. abstention from work. Liberal Judaism, while appreciating the importance of the latter, tends to regard the former as having even greater spiritual value.

The Rabbis drew up a list of 39 prohibited activities which included sowing, ploughing, reaping, grinding, baking, weaving, writing, building, lighting a fire and carrying things from one domain to another (Mish. Shab. 7:2). Subsequently, they extended each of these categories in various directions by way of 'making a fence around the Torah' (Mish. Avot. 1:1). For instance, they prohibited the handling of any object, such as tools and coins, which is normally used in connection with work. It is mainly regarding the relevance of these laws to contemporary life that Orthodox and Progressive Judaism differ. All would agree, however, with the need for Sabbath observance on the traditional 'seventh' day of the week, i.e. Saturday. Since, in ancient times, the day lasted from sunset to sunset, we begin our Sabbath on Friday evening and conclude it on Saturday evening.

Liberal Jews do not necessarily begin their Sabbath at sunset, owing to the difficulties which this creates in the winter months in a society regulated by the clock rather than the sun. Instead, they begin their 24-hour Sabbath rest as soon as the family is assembled in its home on the Friday evening. The mother has the privilege of lighting the two Sabbath candles. Surrounded by her family she welcomes the Sabbath into the home with a meditation (such as can be found in *Service of the Heart*, p. 400) followed by the traditional blessing for the lighting of the Sabbath candles (p. 401). The candles give an atmosphere of sacred joy to the home.

Depending upon the time of the local services, the family might then adjourn to the synagogue to join with other families in welcoming the Sabbath into their community home. On returning to their own home it is customary for the father to pronounce a blessing over the children prior to sitting down for an evening meal. A white tablecloth sets the scene for the festive board, but before the meal is served the ceremony known as the *Kiddush* (Sanctification) is conducted with the aid of wine and the special bread Challah (Hebrew for 'dough'). Details of this ceremony can be found in the prayerbook. It is usually performed by the father of the family and begins with the blessing over the wine (symbol of the 'joy' of the Sabbath day). After all have joined in drinking the wine, the father removes the cloth which has been covering the two Sabbath loaves and recites the blessing over the bread. A piece of bread is handed to every member of the family to symbolize the need for man to share the basic food which God provides for him. If a family is too poor to afford wine, then the bread alone can be used for the Kiddush ceremony. The meal which follows invariably has a festive atmosphere, in addition to providing an opportunity for family reunion, since no member of the family takes on any outside commitment on a Friday night. After the meal, Grace is recited, and this may be followed by the singing of 'table songs' called *Zemirot*.

With regard to the observance of the Sabbath in general, Liberal Judaism does not lay down dogmatic rules except to stress the principle of joyful and peaceful rest coupled with the need for a change from the normal routine of the rest of the week. One should obviously abstain from unnecessary work and from anything that might be transferred to some other day of the week. Consequently, the housewife should not do her shopping on the Saturday. People should do all they can to avoid taking on jobs which demand Saturday work, and they should, if possible, close their business on a Saturday.

If one is forced to work by harsh economic necessity, then an even greater effort should be made to observe the part of the Sabbath day, during which he is not working, in its true spirit. Liberal Judaism believes that riding to the synagogue in private or public transport is not only to be permitted but even encouraged if it will add to the restful spirit of the

Sabbath day, avoiding the need for what may be an excessively long and tiring walk, especially in inclement weather. Similarly, Liberal Judaism permits the use of electrical and gas appliances for any purpose that is essential or likely to contribute to the enjoyment of the Sabbath.

The family should also attend the Sabbath morning service in the synagogue where a congregational Kiddush is often held after the service. An ancient custom, well worth perpetuating, is to look around the synagogue for any stranger who may be present and to extend an invitation to him to return home with you as your Sabbath lunch guest. Many a visitor to a city, many a student far from home and many a lonesome soul has experienced the warmth of Jewish kinship in this way. Saturday lunch should also be a festive meal, preceded by Kiddush and followed by Grace.

Some congregations organize a socio-cultural function, known as *Oneg Shabbat* (Sabbath Joy), on the Friday evening or the Saturday afternoon. This may include the singing of Sabbath songs, the recital of poems and extracts from literature appropriate to the Sabbath, a visiting speaker, and refreshments to add to the convivial atmosphere. This custom was instituted by the famous Jewish poet Bialik in Tel Aviv and has since spread to Jewish communities throughout the world. A third festive meal, especially emphasized by the *Chasidic* sects and known as *Se-udah Shelishit* (third meal) is held by many at the conclusion of the Sabbath.

Just as the Sabbath is welcomed into Jewish homes, so is it ushered out. At the termination of the Sabbath, the family assembles once more for the *Havdalah* (Distinction) ceremony. It is given this name because a prayer is recited which draws a distinction between 'the sacred and the mundane, light and darkness, and the seventh day and the six working days'. Three ceremonial items are used at the *Havdalah* service. First, there is a glass of wine (or any other liquid except water). Second, a lighted taper which dramatizes the distinction between the 'light' of the Sabbath and the relative 'darkness' of the work-a-day week that lies ahead. Third, the family takes turns in smelling spices (*Besamim*) from a spice-box. Some interpret these spices as symbolizing the 'sweetness' of the Sabbath, felt all the more keenly and wistfully as it draws to a close, while others see them as a compensation for the 'additional soul' which comes and departs with the Sabbath. At the end of the ceremony, members of the family greet one another with the words *Shavua Tov*—A good week!

11 Days of Awe

The High Holydays

The Jewish calendar is a lunar one in the sense that it reckons the months from New Moon to New Moon. The New Moon (*Rosh Chodesh:* Head of the month) was celebrated in ancient Israel as a festival, but in modern synagogues it is only commemorated by an announcement being made in the synagogue on the preceding Sabbath that the new month will begin on such-and-such a day of the coming week coupled with a prayer for God's blessing during the month ahead.

In ancient times, the beginning of each month was determined and proclaimed by the Supreme Court in Jerusalem, the so-called Sanhedrin, whenever eye-witnesses reported that they had sighted the New Moon. Since the average duration of a lunar month is 29½ days this could happen during one of two nights: either after the 29th or after the 30th day of the old month. The uncertainty created a problem for the observance of *Rosh Hashanah* (New Year) because it is the one festival which falls on the first day of a month; for if the New Moon should be sighted on the earlier of the two possible nights, several hours of the festival, beginning at dusk, would already have passed unobserved. Therefore it was decided that the month preceding *Rosh Hashanah* should always have only 29 days, and that *Rosh Hashanah* should be observed for two days. Since the other festivals occurred later in the month, they did not present the same problem. However, the communities of the Diaspora found that the emissaries of the Sanhedrin often took some time to reach them so that they were still in doubt as to the correct date of the New Moon. Consequently they added an extra day to all festivals (with the exception of *Yom Kippur*—a day of fasting), and this remains the practice among Orthodox Jews in the Diaspora to this day. Liberal Jews recognizing that this old system became obsolete in the 4th century C.E. when it was superseded by a new, mathematically computed calendar, has abolished the extra days and reverted to the original number of festival days.

To a large extent, the Jewish calendar is based upon that of the Babylonians. Even the names of the months (though the Bible occasionally mentions an older Hebrew one) are of Babylonian origin. For instance, the first month, which falls in the spring, is called *Nissan;* the seventh month, which falls in the autumn, is called *Tishri;* and the 12th month is called *Adar.* Some of the months have 29 days, some 30; two of them may have either 29 or 30 days, a device permitting certain calendrical adjustments, for instance to ensure that *Yom Kippur* never falls on a Friday or a Sunday. Since 12 lunar months come to only 354 days, about 11 days short of the solar year, the effect of having a purely lunar calendar (as in Islam) would be to cause the festivals to 'travel' through the seasons. To avoid this, the Jewish calendar 'intercalates' every two or three years an extra month, called *Adar Sheni* (Second Adar). To be precise, in every 19-year cycle, the 3rd, 6th, 8th, 11th, 14th and 17th are leap years in that sense.

The years themselves are counted according to a medieval reckoning which, on the basis of certain Biblical data and in ignorance of modern cosmology, placed the Creation of the World in the year 3760 B.C.E. Thus *Rosh Hashanah* 1977 inaugurated the Jewish year 5738.

The Days of Awe (*Yamim Nora-im*) consist of *Rosh Hashanah* (New Year) which occurs on the first day of the seventh month (*Tishri*) and *Yom Kippur* (Day of Atonement) which occurs on the 10th day of *Tishri*. The reason for observing the Jewish New Year at the beginning of the *seventh* month is as follows. The ancient Israelites, being predominantly farmers, regarded the autumn harvest as marking the end of one year and the beginning of another. But the Babylonians, whose calendar they adopted during the Exile, held their New Year in the spring, so that for them the spring month of Nisan was the first month. Nevertheless, the older tradition persisted among the Jews and the Jewish New Year remained in the autumn, coinciding with the seventh (Babylonian) month of *Tishri*.

Rosh Hashanah is observed for one day by all U.L.P.S. congregations except one, and for two days by Orthodox Jews in Israel and the Diaspora for reasons explained above. The lighting of the festival candles and the festival *Kiddush* ceremony are carried out in the home; one abstains from unnecessary work; and special services are held in the synagogue. It is a widespread custom to include some apple and honey in the meal to symbolize a 'sweet life' for the family during the coming year, and greeting cards are sent to friends wishing them 'A Happy New Year'.

In the synagogue, the services are longer than usual and concentrate upon the themes of repentance and renewal. During the morning service, the *Shofar* (ram's horn) is sounded as a 'reveille' call to the conscience. It symbolizes the need to rouse ourselves from the spiritual apathy and slumber of the past year to a sense of urgency and reformed conduct. In the Bible the festival is referred to as 'The Day of Trumpet Blowing' (Num. 29:1) and 'The Memorial of Trumpet Blowing' (Lev. 23:24). As it developed, it came to be regarded as the day on which the world was created (R. H. 11a) and as the Day of Judgment on which God judges every human being (Mishnah R. H. 1:2) and decrees his fate accordingly, the decree being 'sealed' 10 days later on *Yom Kippur* (R. Hash. 16a). Implied in this is the poetic fancy that God 'inscribes' the decree in a kind of divine ledger called 'The Book of Life'. Accordingly, the liturgy for the ten days has the recurring prayer, 'Remember us unto life, for You, O king, delight in life; inscribe us in the Book of Life, for Your sake, O God of life'. That is also why the greeting cards, previously referred to, often carry the inscription, *Leshanah tovah tikkatevu vetechatemu* ('May you be inscribed and sealed for a good year'). Some congregations use special white coverings for the Scrolls and the Ark curtains during this period, just as some Ministers wear white robes, to symbolize the aspiration to purity.

In order to make their members aware of the proximity of the penitential season, and to acclimatize them to its atmosphere, some congregations hold a special service of penitential prayers (*selichot*) during the late hours of the Saturday night prior to the New Year. The ten days from *Rosh Hashanah* to *Yom Kippur* are known as *Aseret Yemey Teshuvah* (Ten Days of Penitence). It is a period of spiritual stock-taking, repentance and renewal, and most Liberal Synagogues will not permit festivities (including weddings) to be held during this austere season.

Yom Kippur (Day of Atonement) occurs on the 10th of *Tishri* and is observed for one day both by Orthodox and Progressive Jews. In the Bible it is referred to as a day when 'you shall afflict your souls' (Lev. 16:29, 23:27). It is also described as the day when the High Priest (holding the horns of a 'scapegoat') confessed his own sins, the sins of the priesthood and the sins of the whole nation (Lev. 16:21, Mishnah Yom. 6:2). In modern times, it is devoted almost exclusively to prayer and fasting. We use the occasion to come closer to God and to our fellow beings. The extended worship throughout the day enables us to examine ourselves in the light of God, to confess our failings, and to recognize ways to reformed conduct. We acknowledge our personal sins and our communal sins, and we become aware of our sins of omission as well as our sins of commission. We recognize, too, that to do the right and 'Godly' thing in the future will often involve 'sacrifice' on our part. That is why we make the gesture of 'fasting'—sacrificing food and drink which are so essential to our life—so that we start the year in the spirit in which we intend to continue. Fasting also involves a great deal of self-discipline, and the way in which we respond to the self-imposed fast will give us some indication of the way in which we are likely to respond to other resolutions we have been making during this season. The fast begins officially at sunset and continues until nightfall on the following day. Those who have reason to think that it may be dangerous for their health are exempted from fasting.

A long service is held in the synagogue during the evening when the Festival commences. It is commonly called *Kol Nidrei* from the opening words ('All the vows') of a declaration of medieval origin annulling unfulfillable promises with which the service traditionally begins. Most Liberal synagogues substitute a different text for this declaration but retain the haunting melody which has made the *Kol Nidrei* famous. On the following day, services are held virtually throughout the day. They consist of the Morning service (*Shacharit*), the Additional service (*Musaf*), the Afternoon service (*Minchah*), the Memorial service (*Yizkor*) and the Concluding service (*Ne-ilah*). Some congregations introduce a short break before the Additional service and/or before the Afternoon and Memorial services, so that the atmosphere of worship may not be disturbed by excessively large exits and entries. The Book of Jonah—stressing God's longing for man's repentance—is read during the Afternoon service, and the *Shofar* is sounded at the end of the Concluding service.

Candles are kindled in the home at the commencement of the Festival but there is no Kiddush (because of the fast). Naturally one should abstain from unnecessary work and should attend services in the synagogue. The New Year and the Day of Atonement are known as the 'High Holydays' or the 'Days of Awe' because they are the pinnacle of the annual cycle of Jewish Festivals.

12 Three Times in the Year

The Pilgrimage Festivals

Passover (*Pesach*) is one of the three Pilgrim Festivals (*Shalosh Regalim*) when, in Temple times, every male Jew was expected to make a pilgrimage to Jerusalem: 'Three times a year . . . shall all your males appear before the Lord your God in the place that He will choose' (Deut. 16:16). These Festivals corresponded with the beginning of a particular harvest so that the farmers had the opportunity to give thanks to God for a good crop and to pray for its continuance in the future (Deut. 16:16-17).

Passover appears to be an amalgam of two very ancient festivals, older even than the Exodus from Egypt. One of these was a shepherds' festival celebrating the birth of new lambs in the Spring. The other was a farmers' festival celebrating the beginning of the barley harvest. The first was called *Pesach*, possibly meaning 'to skip', and the second was known as *Chag Hamatzot* (Feast of Unleavened Bread). When the two festivals were combined to become the annual commemoration of the Exodus from Egypt, the word *Pesach* was re-interpreted to refer to the Tenth Plague, when God destroyed the first-born of the Egyptians and 'skipped over' or 'passed over' the houses of the Israelites (Ex. 12:13). Hence the conventional translation of *Pesach* as Passover, and the explanation of the unleavened bread as being due to the haste in which the Israelites left Egypt, so that they did not have time to leaven their dough (Ex. 12:29).

With the destruction of the Temple and the dispersal of the Jewish people, the pastoral, harvest and Temple associations became secondary and the emphasis of the festival was placed upon the past and future liberation of the Jew from bondage. Instead of the pilgrimage to Jerusalem, Jews assembled in their homes and naturally turned their minds to the message of 'freedom'. They recalled memories of their bondage in Egypt and the redemption which followed, and they saw the relevance of these ancient events to their contemporary situation and the hopes they were nursing for future redemption. The liturgy expressed this by referring to the festival as *Zeman Cherutenu* (The Season of our Freedom).

Passover is a seven-day festival (Orthodox Jews in the Diaspora observe eight days) beginning on the 15th *Nisan*, coinciding in the secular calendar with the March-April period. The first and seventh days are observed as 'full festival' (*Yom Tov*) days on which one abstains from un-necessary work, services are held in the synagogue, and *Kiddush* is recited in the home before the evening meal. Candles are kindled in the home at the commencement of the first and last evenings, and the blessing is the same as on the Sabbath except that the last word '*Shabbat*' is replaced by '*Yom Tov*'. Also, on the first evening (Orthodox Jews repeat it on the second evening), a ceremonial family meal and service, known as the *Seder*, is observed in the home. (Some congregations organize a communal *Seder* for those who, for various reasons, are unable to hold one in their own homes.) *Seder* is short for *Seder Haggadah* (Order of narration) and is derived from the Biblical injunction: 'You shall tell your son on that day . . .' (Ex. 13:8), i.e. you should recount the Exodus from Egypt.

The *Seder* can be described as a combination of worship, banqueting, symbolism, religious history and table songs. It is read from a special book called a *Haggadah* (Narration). The whole family, joined by friends, assemble around the table at which they are required to lean (a Roman influence symbo-lizing 'freedom'). Two plates are placed at the head of the table containing a number of symbolic ceremonial items.

On one plate there are three cakes of unleavened bread (*Matzah*) symbolic of the 'haste' in which the Israelites left Egypt. Part of the middle cake, known as the *Aphikoman*, is hidden away and searched for by the children at the end of the meal. It is a word of Greek origin but uncertain meaning. It might mean 'after-dinner entertainment' or 'dessert' (since the eating of it concludes the meal).

On the second plate are a roasted shank-bone (*Zeroa*), symbolic of the Paschal lamb; a roasted egg (*Betzah*), symbolic of the festival burnt offering, or of fertility; bitter herbs (*Maror*), such as horse-radish, symbolic of the bitter life endured by the Israelite slaves; green herbs (*Karpas*), such as watercress or parsley, symbolic of the spring harvest festival; a brown paste made from nuts, raisins, apple, cinammon and wine (*Charoset*), symbolic of the mortar with which the Israelites were forced to make bricks; and a bowl of salt water, into which the parsley is dipped, symbolic of the drowning of the Egyptians in the sea, or of the tears which the slaves shed.

During the course of the evening, each individual drinks four glasses of wine (*Arba Kosot*). There are various explanations of this custom. One refers to the four verbs signifying deliverance in Exodus 6:6-7; another to the four world empires which must pass away before the Messianic Age can begin; a third regards it as a symbol of freedom corresponding to a Roman banquet. One ancient Rabbi, however, believed that five cups should be drunk. Though this view was not generally accepted, it led in the Middle Ages to the custom of pouring out, but not drinking, a fifth cup, known as the 'Cup of Elijah' (*Kos shel Eliyahu*) because Jewish folklore, based on Malachi 3:23, regards Elijah as the harbinger of the Messiah who, among other things, will settle any unresolved problems of Jewish law. This custom may also be understood as sybolizing the thought that, as the fifth cup is filled but not drunk, so the Messianic Age, though anticipated, has not yet come.

Liberal Judaism suggests that, when these ceremonial

items are used during the *Seder*, the head of the table should take time to explain their symbolic significance. In most Liberal Religion Schools a Model *Seder* is held before Passover in order to make the children aware of the full significance of the various parts of the *Seder* service.

Throughout the duration of the festival, on the basis of a repeated prohibition in the Pentateuch, Jews are forbidden to eat, or to keep in their homes, any leaven or any food containing an admixture of leaven. Orthodox Jews tend to observe this prohibition more strictly than Liberal Jews. They even make a ceremony out of the removal of leaven on the eve of the festival, by searching for bread-crumbs (*Bedikat Chametz*) and burning them (*Bi-ur Chametz*) on the following morning.

While the various rituals of the festival play a prominent part in its observance, we should not overlook its universal ethical messages, and our practices should be directed towards opposing tyranny and oppression wherever they occur. We should identify ourselves with all movements which are working to preserve the fundamental human rights of individuals and of groups. The intermediate days of Passover, known as *Chol ha-Mọ-ed* (the non-sacred part of the season) might well be spent in offering our services and material help to those organisations which are involved in the struggle for human rights.

The second of the three Pilgrim festivals is most commonly referred to as *Chag ha-Shavuot* (The Feast of Weeks) or simply *Shavuot* (Weeks), in allusion to the fact that it was to be observed seven weeks after Passover. The ancient Israelites counted 49 days from the second day of *Pesach*, and the 50th was observed as a festival. Since the Greek word for 50th is Pentecost, the festival is often referred to by that name. In the Bible it is described purely as a nature festival celebrating the wheat harvest; but in post-Biblical times it was given a historical significance. This was derived from the statement that the Israelites entered the wilderness of Sinai 'in the third month' after their departure from Egypt (Ex. 19:1).

In other words, *Shavuot* became the festival of the Sinaitic revelation. Accordingly, the Jewish liturgy refers to it as *Zeman Mattan Toratenu* (The Season of the Giving of our Torah). As *Pesach* is the festival of Freedom, so *Shavuot* is the festival of Law.

It occurs on the 6th *Sivan*, coinciding in the secular calendar with the May-June period, and it lasts for one day (Diaspora Orthodox Jews observe two days). The lighting of the festival candles and the festival *Kiddush* ceremony are carried out in the home; one abstains from unnecessary work; and special services are held in the synagogue. It is a widespread custom in many Jewish homes to consume dairy foods on this festival.

In the synagogue one notices flowers and plants which are intended to remind us of its original association with Nature, and the Ten Commandments are appropriately recited from the Scroll during the morning service. The Book of Ruth is read on this festival—partly because of its harvest setting, partly because Ruth's conversion to Judaism may be considered analagous to the Israelites' acceptance of the Torah at Sinai, and partly on account of a legend that King David, who was Ruth's great-grandson, died on *Shavuot*. Another custom, which originated among the Kabbalists in the Middle Ages, is to spend the whole night of the festival studying selections from the Bible and post-Biblical Jewish literature. For this purpose a special book is used, called a *Tikkun* (Arrangement), and the all-night ceremony is called *Tikkun Leyl Shavuot* (Arrangement of readings for the night of Pentecost). This custom has been revived in a revised form by a number of Liberal Jewish congregations in recent years. Many Liberal synagogues arrange their annual Confirmation service (referred to in another chapter) on this festival since the Israelites committed themselves to God at Sinai (Ex. 19:8, 24:3).

The third of the Pilgrim festivals, *Sukkot* (Tabernacles or Booths), commemorates the conclusion of the entire harvest, both fruit and grain, and is the only one of the original harvest festivals which is still observed primarily as such. It begins five days after the Day of Atonement, on the 15th *Tishri*, corresponding in the secular calendar with the September-October period. The Bible states that it should be a seven-day festival (Lev. 23:34) with an Eighth Day of Solemn Assembly (*Shemini Atzeret*) added (Lev. 23:36). Orthodox Jews in the Diaspora add a ninth day, the Rejoicing in the Law (*Simchat Torah*), but Liberal Jews combine the latter with the eighth and final day of the festival. The first and last days are observed as full festival days with the lighting of the festival candles and the festival *Kiddush* being recited in the home; abstaining from unnecessary work; and special services being held in the synagogue.

The principal feature of the observance of *Sukkot*, from which it derives its name, is the custom of dwelling in booths during its seven days. The reason given in the Bible is 'in order that future generations may know that I made the Israelites dwell in booths when I brought them out of the land of Egypt' (Lev. 23:43). But since desert-travellers do not use booths, and since in any case this interpretation fails to explain the date of the festival, it is more likely that the booths hark back to those erected by the farmers during the harvest, or else to those erected in Jerusalem to accommodate the pilgrims. However that may be, many Jewish families still observe the custom of building a booth (*Sukkah*) in their garden, and taking their meals in it during the festival if not actually sleeping in it. It is a temporary structure with no permanent roof. The ceiling is usually made of interlocking twigs and greenery symbolizing man's dependence upon God, and fruit is hung from the ceiling. Most synagogues erect a *Sukkah*, using the fruit, vegetables and greenery brought by the members, and *Kiddush* is held in the *Sukkah* after the festival services.

The other main feature of *Sukkot* is the use of the Four Species (*Arba-ah Minim*). These are first mentioned in Leviticus 23:40 and were later interpreted to mean (a) the

Lulav (Palm-branch) tied together with two willow branches and three myrtle branches, and (b) the *Etrog* (Citron). They may be regarded as representing the variety of nature. The custom is to carry them in procession, and to wave them in all directions during the recitation of the *Hallel* Psalms. On the Sabbath during *Sukkot* it is traditional to read the Book of Ecclesiastes (*Kohelet*) which sees man as an integral part of nature.

Sukkot is a joyful festival and is referred to in the liturgy as *Zeman Simchatenu* (The Season of our Gladness), going back to the Biblical injunction: 'You shall rejoice on your festival...' (Deut. 16:14). This joy is expressed to the full on the last day of the festival known as *Simchat Torah* (Rejoicing of the Law). This is the occasion when we complete the annual cycle of readings from the Torah. We read the final verses from the Book of Deuteronomy (*Devarim*), but because the reading of sacred literature should never cease, we immediately read from another Scroll the opening verses of the Book of Genesis (*Bereshit*). Two members of the congregation are afforded the honour of being called up when these portions are read, and they are known as the Bridegroom of the Law (*Chatan Torah*) and the Bridegroom of the Beginning (*Chatan Bereshit*). Many congregations also include a Procession of the Scrolls during which a number of circuits (*Hakkafot*) are made of the synagogue, with congregants taking turns to carry the Scrolls. In many synagogues, too, 'all the children' are called together to a reading from the Scroll and a number of joyful songs are sung to express the happiness of the occasion. At the *Kiddush* after the service, the children are given generous helpings of fruit and sweets.

While the harvest festival of *Sukkot* is an occasion for great joy and thanksgiving, we should not overlook our responsibility to that large proportion of the world's population which is suffering from hunger and malnutrition. There can be no better time to identify ourselves actively with such organizations as the War on Want than on *Sukkot*.

13 Joy and Gladness

The minor feasts and fasts

A 'minor' festival is of less significance than the 'major' festivals which have been described in previous chapters. Not being in the full sense a *Yom Tov*, it does not require abstention from work and the *Kiddush* is not recited in the home.

The minor festival of *Chanukkah* (Dedication) is based upon the victorious rebellion of the Maccabees against the Greco-Syrian King Antiochus Epiphanes who, having occupied Judea, sought to replace Judaism with a pagan religion. The full story can be found in the Books of the Maccabees in the Apocrypha. The festival celebrates the rededication of the Temple in 165 B.C.E. after it had been recaptured from the Syrians, cleansed, and restored for Jewish worship. It celebrates the victory of the 'few' over the 'many', giving encouragement to all minorities to stick to their principles, for right will triumph in the end. It also recalls the heroic sacrifice and resistance of the Maccabees and their followers which ensured the survival of monotheism in general and Judaism in particular.

The festival begins on the 25th *Kislev* (coinciding with the November-December period in the secular calendar), and lasts for eight days. In the home a special candlestick, known as a *Chanukkiyyah*, is used on each of the eight evenings of the festival. The candlestick has eight branches for candles, and a ninth known as the 'Servant' (*Shammash*) is used to light the others. On the first evening, the 'servant' lights one candle (which is allowed to burn out), while a service is conducted as found in the Prayer Book (pp. 413-417). This continues on

140

each of the eight evenings, an additional candle being lit each night until all eight candles burn together on the last night. A Talmudic legend attempts to explain this ceremony by referring to the 'miracle' of a cruse of oil burning for eight days in the Temple instead of the anticipated one day, but the real origin of this custom is probably linked with the pagan Winter Solstice festivities which occur at the same time.

In modern times, the kindling of the *Chanukkiyyah* can be regarded as symbolically teaching such lessons as the following: that our faith should grow from small beginnings until it shines in its full splendour; that the power of our religious message (like the light of the *Chanukkiyyah*) is so much stronger when one is joined by another, and then another, etc., until there are no gaps and no absentees; that as the 'servant' candle brings light to all the other candles, so the Jew, as God's servant, should bring light to all the people of the world.

It is customary to arrange parties for children on this festival and to give them presents. One of the favourite games involves the use of a top (*Sevivon*) on which are written the Hebrew letters N (*nun*), G (*gimmel*), H (*hay*), SH (*shin*), which some interpret as being the first letters of the words which mean 'A great miracle occurred there', or representing the number of coins (or nuts, or sweets) which must be put in or taken out of the kitty. The synagogue services during *Chanukkah*, as on the *Shalosh Regalim*, include the recitation of the *Hallel* (Psalms of praise).

The minor festival of *Purim* (Lots) is celebrated on the 14th *Adar* (coinciding with the February-March period). In a leap year it is celebrated on 14th *Adar Sheni*. The story of this festival is to be found in the Bible in the Book of Esther. It describes how Queen Esther saved the Jews of Persia from the destruction which the wicked Haman plotted to bring upon them after casting lots to choose the most propitious day. It was on that same day, the story goes, that the plot was foiled and 'The Jews had light and gladness, and joy and honour' (8:16). A critical analysis of this book has led to the conclusion that it is unhistorical as well as lacking in religious motivation and ethical sensitivity. These reasons have led a few Liberal Jewish congregations wholly or largely to disregard this minor festival.

However, most congregations do pay some attention to this festival, particularly by reading extracts from the Book of Esther on the preceding Sabbath, if not on the festival itself, and holding children's parties. While these congregations do not necessarily reject the above mentioned criticisms, they tend to feel that the story of Esther, even if fictional, does serve as a prototype of the kind of experience which the Jewish people have undergone all too frequently in the course of their history; that the objectionable features of the Book of Esther are largely neutralized by the jocular carnival spirit in which the festival is celebrated; and that there is psychological value in having just such a light-hearted 'mini-festival' among the more serious feasts and fasts of the Jewish year. The celebrations mostly consist of parties, games, fancy-dress parades, giving presents to the poor, etc. In modern Israel, the day is given over to processions and a carnival atmosphere. Many people like to eat special triangular poppy-seed cakes (*Hamantaschen*). In the synagogue, the Scroll (*Megillah*) of Esther is recited, during which the children often stamp their feet, or turn their rattles or 'greggers', at every mention of the name of the villain Haman.

It may be appropriate here to refer to the *Sefirah* (counting) which takes place during the 50 days that separate *Pesach* from *Shavuot*. On the second day of *Pesach* a sheaf (*Omer*) of newly-harvested barley was offered in the Temple, and from that day 49 days were counted until *Shavuot*, the 50th day, on which two loaves of leavened bread were offered. Orthodox Jews still count the days during which, for instance, weddings are disallowed. The reason is not clear—it probably derives from some pagan superstition—but an attempt has been made to link it with the death of a large number of Rabbi

Akiva's students during this period mentioned in the Talmud (Yev. 62b). An exception to the austerity is made on the 33rd day of the counting of the Omer (*Lag ba-Omer*) which was described as the 'scholars' festival' because, on the basis of an incorrect reading of the Talmudic passage, the plague was believed to have stopped miraculously on that day.

While ignoring the superstititious elements of these observances, some Liberal Jewish congregations have nevertheless revived the custom of 'counting' the days between *Pesach* and *Shavuot* to emphasize the inter-connection of these festivals, the festival of 'freedom' and the festival of 'law'. Freedom, by itself, could easily degenerate into licence and anarchy. It needs to be disciplined by law in order to ensure the protection of freedom for all. Similarly law by itself could easily lead to totalitarianism and the police state. It needs to recognize personal freedom if it is not to become oppressive. The Rabbis called *Shavuot* by the name *Atzeret* (which can be translated as 'completion') because it completes the process started at *Pesach*. One Liberal Jewish congregation asks its members to bring gifts of tinned foods on each of the days of the *Sefirah* and they are then given to worthy causes on *Shavuot*.

Another minor festival is the New Year for the Trees (*Rosh Hashanah la-Ilanot*) which is observed on 15th *Shevat* (*Tu Bi-Shevat*), coinciding with the January-February period. This custom is first mentioned in the Mishnah (R. Hash 1:1). In Israel, at this time, the winter is passing and the sap is beginning to fill the trees bringing the spring blossoms. Children are particularly encouraged to go out and plant saplings. In this country it provides an opportunity to publicize the work of the Jewish National Fund (*Keren Kayemet LeYisrael*) with regard to land reclamation and afforestation.

The most significant event in our generation has undoubtedly been the establishment of the State of Israel. The anniversary on the 5th *Iyyar* (coinciding with the April-May period) is observed as Independence Day (*Yom ha-Atzmaut*), and many congregations hold services of thanksgiving, parties, etc. The Union of Liberal and Progressive Synagogues was one of the first Jewish religious organizations to compile a special Order of Service for this occasion.

In conclusion, although it is not a day of 'joy and gladness' we might make mention of the saddest day in the Jewish year, *Tish'ah b'Av* (the 9th of *Av*). It commemorates the destruction of both the first and the second Temples as well as other tragedies of Jewish history. It is observed as a 24-hour fast, and the Book of Lamentations is read. Some Liberal Jews prefer to commemorate other days of Jewish suffering such as *Crystal* Night (9th November) when the Nazis launched their campaign against the Jews by burning synagogues and arresting and maltreating many Jews, or Holocaust Memorial Day (*Yom ha-Sho-ah*) on 27th *Nisan*, the anniversary of the Warsaw Ghetto uprising. Three other fast-days, the 17th of *Tammuz*, the 3rd of *Tishri* and the 10th of *Tevet*, commemorate various events relating to the Babylonian conquest of Judea and the fall of the first Temple. But though these are already alluded to in the Bible, few people observe them nowadays.

14 All your Children shall be Taught of the Lord

Rituals relating to birth and to adolescence

'All your children shall be taught of the Lord, and great shall be the peace of your children' (Is. 54:13). On this famous verse in the Book of Isaiah, the Rabbis commented: 'Read not *banayich*, your children, but *bonayich*, your builders' (Ber. 64a). Jews have always understood that the perpetuation of the Jewish heritage depends decisively on its successful transmission from generation to generation, and therefore from parents to children, who are the 'builders' of the Jewish future. This concern has expressed itself in the Jewish rituals associated with childhood from birth to adolescence.

When a child is born, it is important that the parents be given an opportunity to give thanks to God and to seek His guidance in the correct upbringing of the child. That is why a special ceremony (private or public) is held in a Liberal synagogue as soon as the parents are able to bring the child. Standing before the open Ark the mother recites a prayer of thanksgiving for recovery from childbirth, and asks God to guide her and her husband to lead their child 'in the way of righteousness and holiness' and that their child might grow up to be 'loyal to Judaism and a worthy member of the Jewish community'. The Minister then recites a prayer in which the name of the child is mentioned, and the ceremony concludes with the ancient priestly benediction (*Service of the Heart*, pp. 432-5).

Many Liberal Jewish parents follow the ancient custom of giving the child a 'Hebrew' name. Among Ashkenazi Jews the prevailing practice is to name the child after a deceased relative, while Sefardi Jews often give the child the name of a living relative. Liberal Judaism applies no such limitation. In Orthodox Judaism the name of a girl is given when the father is called to the Reading of the Law in the synagogue and a special prayer (*Mi She-berach*) is recited. The name of the boy is given at his circumcision (*B'rit Milah*).

Circumcision is a simple operation by which the foreskin of the penis is removed. This is a widespread custom. Apart from Jews, it is also practised by Muslims and various other societies. Nowadays it is commonly justified on medical grounds, and it is claimed that it prevents certain diseases such as phimosis and cancer of the penis. But it is also a very ancient custom going back to pre-historic times. What motivated it originally is not clear. Perhaps it was once regarded as a token child sacrifice, but more probably it was at first (as, in some primitive societies, it still is) a puberty rite, i.e. a ceremony of initiation into manhood. However that may be, in Judaism it was interpreted as a sign of the Covenant—hence it is known in Hebrew as *B'rit Milah*, 'The Covenant of Circumcision'—i.e. as a lifelong reminder to the Jew that he is a member of the Jewish people, with all the responsibilities which that fact entails. As such, it is especially associated with Abraham (Gen. 17:9-14), and also with Elijah, the champion of the Covenant (I Kings, 19:14). Liberal Jews observe the practice as 'a matter of conforming to a particularly ancient Jewish practice, deeply embedded in Jewish emotion'.

The operation is normally performed on the eighth day of the baby's life, even if it happens to be a Sabbath or a festival, and by a person, known as a *Mohel* (circumciser), who has been specially trained in the traditional Jewish way of doing it. Some parents, however, prefer to have it done by a surgeon, or by a person who has both qualifications. The full traditional ritual (which some Liberal Jews prefer to curtail or dispense with) is as follows. First, the child is welcomed with the words *Baruch ha-ba* (Blessed be he who comes). Then the father declares his readiness to fulfil the obligation to have his son circumcised. The *Mohel* next places the child on a seat known as 'The Chair of Elijah' and recites some Scriptural verses. Then the child is held by a male relative or friend, known as the *Sandek* (a Hebraized Greek word of uncertain meaning), while the *Mohel* performs the operation, preceded by a short benediction, 'We praise You, O Lord our God, King of the universe, who have sanctified us by Your commandments and commanded us to initiate our sons into the Covenant of our forefather Abraham,' to which those present respond, 'As this child has entered into the Covenant, so may he enter into a life of Torah, marriage and good deeds'. The ceremony concludes with a few more prayers and Scripture verses, whereupon all drink a cup of wine as a symbol of joy. As on all happy occasions, the family is congratulated with the phrase *Mazzal Tov* (which originally meant 'a good constellation' but has come to mean 'good luck' or 'congratulations').

In ancient times, the first-born of every Jewish family was supposed to be consecrated to serve in the priesthood (Ex. 13:2). Later, this became the privilege of the tribe of Levi (Num. 3:11-13). Then it became customary for the father to 'redeem' his first-born by paying a ransom of five shekels to a member of the priesthood (Num. 18:15-16). This ceremony, known as *Pidyon ha-Ben* (Redemption of the son), is still practised among Orthodox Jews. It is performed on the 31st day of the boy's life, but does not apply if either parent is known, or presumed, to be descended from the ancient priests (*Cohanim*) or Levites. Liberal Jews consider the ceremony no longer meaningful, and do not practise it. An idea worth considering, however, is to use the opportunity to establish a 'savings fund' on the birth of a child, in the hope that there will be enough money in that fund to pay for that child to visit the State of Israel when it reaches *Bar/Bat Mitzvah* or Confirmation.

We have explained in a previous chapter the need to provide religious education for children (of both sexes) virtually from birth. Despite the attempt to provide a solid

147

foundation, it must be admitted that adolescence often becomes a time of confusion and rebellion. Judaism rightly concentrates upon the adolescent during this crucial period of his life and seeks to bind him even more closely to his religious faith. It is interesting to note, however, that 'adolescence', as a period between childhood and adulthood, was not given official recognition. In ancient times a child was deemed to become an adult virtually 'overnight', with the onset of puberty, Rabbinic Law, accordingly, fixed the age of majority at the age when, on average, that biological change begins to take place—13 in the case of boys, 12 in the case of girls. To be precise, a boy was considered a minor (*Katan*) until his 13th birthday; on the following day he became a major (*Gadol*) and therefore a *Bar Mitzvah* (Son of Duty), i.e., subject to all the obligations applicable to Jewish men. A girl was considered a minor (*Ketannah*) until her 12th birthday; then she became a major (*Gedolah*), but for another six months she was known as a 'girl' (*Na-arah*) before acquiring the status of a 'mature woman' (*Bogeret*).

Surprisingly, in view of the customs of many other societies, Judaism, during the greater part of its history, had no official 'coming of age' ceremonies. Only in the late Middle Ages (14th-16th centuries) did the *Bar Mitzvah* ceremony establish itself. According to modern Orthodox practice the young man, at the Sabbath Morning service following his 13th birthday, demonstrates his competence to fulfil the obligations and privileges of a grown-up male Jew by being 'called up' to read all or part of the *Parashah* (weekly Torah portion) and perhaps also the *Haftarah* (reading from the Prophets). After the service there is usually a festive meal and celebration during which the boy may further demonstrate his learning by delivering a discourse on some Talmudic subject, although it is more likely nowadays that he will make a speech thanking everybody for their presents! It should be emphasized, however, that a Jewish boy's attainment of his majority does not depend upon this *Bar Mitzvah* ceremony—it is just a legal 'fact' on account of his age. Similarly, girls attain their majority at 12, even though Rabbinic Judaism never devised a coming-of-age ceremony for them.

Progressive Judaism, from its inception in the early 19th century, objected to the traditional *Bar Mitzvah* ceremony because it was confined to boys and because 13 seemed too young an age for a mature understanding of Judaism to have been achieved. There was also the pitiful sight of 13-year-old boys deserting their Religion Schools as soon as they had become *Bar Mitzvah* and developing into religious 'illiterates'. Progressive Judaism, therefore, prolonged the process of formal Jewish education by two or three years and instituted, at its end, a group graduation ceremony for boys and girls together, called 'Confirmation'. This must not be confused with the Christian sacrament of Confirmation. It was given this name because the boys and girls 'confirm' the pledge of loyalty to the Covenant which the Israelites, assembled at Sinai, made on behalf of the entire Jewish people, present and future. For the same reason, many Progressive Jewish communities like to combine the Confirmation ceremony with the festival of *Shavuot*, celebrating the Sinaitic Revelation. Some congregations use a Hebrew term such as *Kabbalat Mitzvah* (Acceptance of Duty) or *Ben Torah/Bat Torah* (Son of the Torah/Daughter of the Torah), instead of 'Confirmation'.

A few Liberal Jewish congregations continue to replace the *Bar Mitzvah* ceremony by Confirmation. However, in recent years, most Liberal Jewish congregations, while insisting upon the Confirmation ceremony as the final goal, have given the option of a *Bar/Bat Mitzvah* ceremony in addition under certain conditions. The latter congregations would argue that six hundred years of Jewish practice cannot easily be eradicated from the Jewish consciousness. They would admit that the *Bar Mitzvah* ceremony had deteriorated over the years, but they would argue that new conditions might improve the situation. These conditions permit a girl to become *Bat Mitzvah* at the age of 13 on exactly the same terms as a boy becoming *Bar Mitzvah*. They are only permitted to have the religious ceremony (on the Sabbath following their 13th birthday) if they give a pledge in writing to continue their religious education until their Confirmation. They must also give evidence of regular attendance at Religion School and at services for a specified number of years prior to *Bar/Bat Mitzvah*, and they are only permitted to recite, during the ceremony, words which they fully understand. During the ceremony itself they are told that, far from concluding their Jewish studies, they are about to begin an intensive course leading to Confirmation, and that they will no longer be treated as young children but as maturing adolescents. It should be added that a number of Orthodox synagogues have seen the virtue of the Progressive Jewish approach to this matter and endeavoured both to prolong the Religion School years and to introduce some kind of *Bat Mitzvah* ceremony for girls.

15 The Voice of the Bridegroom and the Voice of the Bride

Rituals relating to marriage

We have already described in chapter 3 the importance of the marriage bond in the context of family life and the home. In this chapter we will deal primarily with the practices associated with the marriage ceremony itself. The reader is strongly urged to read Rabbi John Rayner's booklet, *A Guide to Jewish Marriage*, for a detailed discussion of all aspects of Jewish marriage from a Liberal Jewish viewpoint.

First, it must be stressed that a Jewish marriage ceremony does not have to take place in a synagogue. It can be performed anywhere and, according to Liberal Judaism, can be held on any day except the Sabbath, the Festivals, the Ten Days of Penitence and *Tish'ah b'Av*. Second, only 'persons professing the Jewish religion' are eligible for a Jewish marriage ceremony in this country. Not only is this because the English civil laws demand it, but also because it would be inconsistent for a non-Jewish bride or bridegroom to undertake obligations according to the teachings of the Jewish religion. With regard to the Liberal Jewish interpretation of who is a person 'professing the Jewish religion', Jewish status is afforded to (a) anyone born of Jewish parents, and who has not embraced some other faith, (b) anyone born of one Jewish parent and able to provide evidence of having been brought up only in the Jewish faith (as opposed to the Rabbinic ruling that only the child of a Jewish mother is Jewish), (c) anyone converted to Judaism by a responsible religious authority, (d) anyone adopted in infancy by Jewish parents and brought up as a Jew.

Tracing the history of the Jewish marriage ceremony, it began with the engagement (*Shidduchin*). This was followed by *Kiddushin*, which literally means 'Consecration' but is commonly translated as 'Betrothal', and consisted of the Bridegroom, in the presence of two witnesses, giving the Bride an object of a certain minimum value (which became the ring) while declaring her to be his wife. From that moment they were legally married, but they did not live together until the next and final stage, known as *Nissu-in* (Carrying-away or Wedding), usually a year later, when the marriage was consummated in the bridal chamber (*Chuppah*), and a joyful feast ensued. In the Middle Ages, the two stages of *Kiddushin* and *Nissu-in* became combined to form the Jewish marriage service as we now know it.

First, the bridegroom (*Chatan*) enters and stands under a canopy (*Chuppah*—named after the ancient bridal chamber). Then the bride (*Kallah*) enters and stands on his right. The parents, best man, and bridesmaids stand on either side. After the singing of 'Blessed be he who comes in the name of the Lord; we bless you from the House of the Lord' (Psalm 118:26) and the 100th Psalm, the Rabbi asks the bridegroom and the bride to declare their willingness to marry each other and their acceptance of the responsibilities of marriage. This is followed by the singing of 'He who is mighty, blessed and great above all beings, may He bless the bridegroom and the bride'. At this point the Rabbi usually gives an address. Then comes the betrothal benediction (which is tradition-ally recited over a cup of wine, though this is not generally done in Liberal synagogues), whereupon the bridegroom places the ring on the bride's finger and says to her: 'You are betrothed to me by this ring according to the law of Moses and Israel'. In Liberal Judaism the bride usually repeats this declaration, with or without giving the bride-groom a ring in return. The Rabbi then reads out the religious marriage certificate, known as the *Ketubbah*. In its traditional form, this is an Aramaic document including certain financial clauses which were originally designed to give the wife a measure of security in case the husband should divorce or predecease her. In Liberal Judaism it is a certificate in Hebrew and in English and omits the financial clauses.

Next, the 'seven benedictions' (*Sheva Berachot*) are recited over a cup of wine, from which the bridegroom and the bride sip to symbolize that in future 'you will share all things even as you share this cup of wine'. The last and longest of the seven benedictions includes one of the many phrases of the Jewish marriage ritual, which is taken from the Bible: 'The voice of joy and the voice of gladness, the voice of the bridegroom and the voice of the bride' (Jer. 33:11).

The bridegroom then breaks a glass underfoot. While this medieval custom was probably based upon the superstition that the breaking glass would drive away envious evil spirits (is that why people commonly call out *Mazzal Tov*—good luck—at this point?), other interpretations have now been placed upon this ritual. Some suggest that a 'jarring' note is introduced into the happy occasion to remind the bridegroom and bride that life consists of both pleasant and unpleasant experiences. Another interpretation is that it brings home to the couple the fragility of marriage. Just as one blow can shatter the glass, so can the peace and harmony of the home be shattered by a single act of infidelity. Yet another explanation is that it reminds the couple of the destruction of the Temple in Jerusalem. The Temple used to be the centre of Jewish religious inspiration, but since its destruction, every Jewish home must become a Temple of purity and holiness. The couple, who are about to set up a home together, are reminded of their obligation to turn it into a small sanctuary. The service concludes with the ancient priestly benediction and the singing of the 150th Psalm.

In many Liberal synagogues, it is a custom to invite the bride to kindle the Sabbath candles at the Sabbath eve service prior to her marriage, and for the bridegroom to be called to the Torah or opening the Ark on the preceding Sabbath morning. Similarly they may be honoured by the congregation whenever they celebrate the anniversary of their marriage.

After their honeymoon, the couple return to their home—to their sanctuary. Just as Solomon performed a dedication ceremony when the first Temple was completed (I Kings 8), so is it customary for Jews to perform a ceremony of dedication, known as *Chanukkat ha-Bayit* (Dedication of the House), before they enter their new home. The Prayer Book contains a suggested Order of Service (pp. 425-428). This does not necessarily have to be conducted by a Minister; on the contrary, it is more important that the head of the home should officiate at the dedication of his family's sanctuary in which he will have to preside on numerous other religious occasions.

The ceremony includes the fixing of the *Mezuzah* in fulfilment of the Scriptural injunction: 'You shall write them on the doorposts (*Mezuzot*) of your house, and upon your gates'. The *Mezuzah* is a cylinder containing a parchment scroll inscribed with the Scriptural passages Deuteronomy 6:4-9 and 11:13-21. It is fixed on the upper part of the right-hand door-post, slanting upwards and inwards. Traditionally, every living room door should have one, though many Jews, especially Progressive Jews, content themselves with having one fixed to the main entrance to their home. The purpose of the *Mezuzah* is to remind the occupants of the home, whenever they enter or leave it, of their religious obligations as Jews.

Since one of the first decisions a couple have to make, as they begin their married life, concerns their eating habits, it may be appropriate here to deal with the Dietary Laws (*Kashrut*). First, these laws state that certain species are forbidden. Among quadrupeds, only those may be eaten which both part the hoof and chew the cud, thus excluding, among others, the pig and the hare. Among creatures that live in water, only fish having both fins and scales are permitted, thus excluding eels as well as lobsters and the like. Regarding birds, there is no general rule, but only those which the Bible specifically permits may be eaten. All other animals, such as insects and reptiles, are forbidden, with the exception of locusts.

An animal belonging to a permitted species is subject to further restrictions. It may not be eaten if it has died of itself or if it is injured; and it must be correctly slaughtered. The Rabbis devised a particular method of slaughter in order (a) to cause the minimum of pain and (b) to allow as much blood as possible to escape, since the consumption of blood was considered forbidden. This method of slaughter, which applies only to quadrupeds and birds, is called *Shechitah*, and the slaughterer, who has been specially trained and qualified, is called a *Shochet*. After slaughter, the carcass is meticulously inspected for any sign of injury or disease. If such a sign is found, it is declared *Terefah*—i.e. forbidden. Next, certain parts of the carcass are removed, since the Bible forbids certain fats, as well as 'the sinew that shrank'—a process known as 'porging'. A *kosher* butcher guarantees that his meat measures up to all these requirements. However, when the meat reaches the housewife, unless it is to be roasted, it is soaked in water for half an hour, then salted for one hour and finally rinsed. This process is commonly called '*kashering*', and its purpose is to drain away still more of the blood.

The meat may then be eaten, but there is still another restriction to be noted. Because the Bible says in three different places, 'You shall not boil a kid in its mother's milk', the Rabbis prohibited all mixing of meat and milk products. Not only may they not be cooked or eaten together, but after eating meat one should wait several hours (six, according to the strictest authorities) before consuming anything made of milk. Conversely, after consuming a dairy product, it is sufficient to rinse one's mouth before eating meat. In order to avoid any violation of this law, strictly Orthodox households keep separate pots and pans, as well as crockery and cutlery, for the two kinds of food, known in Yiddish as *fleischig* (meaty) and *milchig* (milky) respectively.

155

These dietary laws have been defended in various ways. Orthodox Judaism asserts that they are God's commandments and their obligatory character is, therefore, not in question. By way of explanation, they would either claim that they have some hygienic value, or they would assert that they teach us self-discipline.

Liberal Jews would not accept the claim of the divine origin of these laws, and would place their hygienic value more in the past than the present. With regard to *Shechitah*, the main question is whether it is still, as undoubtedly it once was, the most humane method of slaughter. While many of the leading experts do consider it as humane as any other method of slaughter, not all take that view. If, therefore, at some future date, all experts could agree that there is a more humane method of slaughter than *Shechitah*, Liberal Judaism would be obliged to advocate that method, whether or not it accorded with Rabbinic law, on the ground that the general ethical principle of *Tza-ar Ba-aley Chayyim* (i.e. the avoidance of inflicting unnecessary suffering upon animals) must be given priority over ritualistic legislation.

With regard to the law that 'you shall not boil a kid in its mother's milk', already Maimonides conjectured in the Middle Ages, and modern archaeological discoveries have confirmed the conjecture, that it was originally directed against the imitation of a particular pagan fertility rite. That being so, it is hard rationally to justify the elaborate Rabbinic legislation concerning the separation of meat and milk.

It appears that a Liberal Jew may adopt one of the two following policies with regard to the Dietary laws. (1) He may say, 'Although I do not regard them as being in all respects divinely commanded or rationally justified, nevertheless I accept them *in toto* as one of the 'folkways' of the Jewish people and/or as a valuable exercise in self-discipline'. Or (2) he may say, 'The question, what to eat and what not to eat, has religious and ethical significance only in so far as it involves considerations of health (since we have a duty to keep ourselves fit) and considerations of humaneness (since we have a duty not to inflict avoidable suffering on animals). Therefore I shall keep those laws, but only those, which serve either of these purposes; but as to which these are, I must be guided by modern science rather than ancient folklore'. Liberal Judaism regards either of these views as legitimate and therefore leaves it to the individual to choose between them. Thus there is no uniformity of practice among Liberal Jews in this matter, but all would agree that the main thrust of Judaism is directed to purposes more important that eating habits. It would be advisable, however, for a couple to decide upon their dietary procedure well before the bride ventures upon serving her first meal after the honeymoon.

16 Your God shall be my God

The acceptance of sincere proselytes

Abraham might well be regarded as the first convert to
Judaism. Had he not left his idol-worshipping background in
order to serve the one spiritual God, there might well have
been no Judaism. Dr. Claude Montefiore has pointed out
that 'in Rabbinic Hebrew the proselyte is called *ger*, whereas
in Biblical Hebrew the *ger* is the resident alien (A.V., R.V.
"stranger"). So all the laws in the Pentateuch enjoining
kindness to the *ger* are by the Rabbis applied to the proselyte'.
Thus, 'There shall be one law for the native and for the *ger*',
and 'The *ger* who dwells with you shall be as the homeborn
and you shall love him as yourself'.

The Book of Ruth is the classic Biblical example of
the acceptance of the righteous proselyte, when the
Moabitish woman Ruth declares to her Judean mother-
in-law Naomi, 'your people shall be my people and your
God my God' (1:17). It is often asserted that the Book of
Ruth was written to counter the 'anti-foreign' attitude
contained within the Books of Ezra and Nehemiah, which
condemned those Jews who had married 'the women of
Ashdod, Ammon and Moab' (Neh. 13:23), and ordered
them to put away their foreign wives (Ezra 10:3, 11, Neh.
13:3), because these women had led them to sin. But neither
Ezra nor Nehemiah makes any reference to proselytes, and it
is therefore possible that they were simply opposed to
intermarriage. In any event, as Rabbi Albert Goldstein has
pointed out, 'The stand which Ezra-Nehemiah took against
foreigners as such is contrary to that of their Biblical pre-

decessors, and it did not go unchallenged by their literary successors'.

While there has always been a tension between particularism and universalism in Judaism, as in other religions, there is no doubt that the Hebrew prophets were in favour of spreading the message of Judaism as exemplified by Isaiah: 'I will give you for a light unto the nations, that My salvation may be unto the end of the earth' (Is. 49:6). Or, as Rabbi Bernard Bamberger put it, 'The message of a universal God, of a universal law, and of a humanity that is already one in essence and in the end of days shall become one in actual brotherhood—this message could not remain the exclusive possession of one nation without hopeless contradiction. One who believes in humanity cannot become an isolationist and retire behind iron walls to enjoy the splendid humanitarian vision in cloistered exclusiveness'.

While some people have tried to argue that there were mixed views regarding the value of proselytes in Rabbinic times, Rabbi Bamberger, in his excellent book *Proselytism in the Talmudic Period*, has shown that the Rabbis were overwhelmingly in favour of proselytes, and that very little weight should be attached to contrary statements which were so exceptional as to be almost negligible. In this light we should regard such statements as those which referred to proselytes as an affliction, or which complained that they had hindered the coming of the Messiah (Nid. 13b). Similarly we should understand that when Rabbi Chelbo declared 'Converts are as troublesome to Israel as the plague of leprosy' (Yev. 47b) he was living at a time when the Roman Empire had just adopted Christianity and had issued an edict making conversion to Judaism a punishable offence both for the converter and for the converted.

The predominant Rabbinic viewpoint is expressed in such statements as that of Eleazar ben Pedat, 'God scattered Israel among the nations for the sole end that proselytes should be numerous among them' (Pes. 87b), or that of Simeon ben Lakish who said that the proselyte who has come of his own free will is dearer to God than all the crowds of Israelites who stood around Mount Sinai, since the latter accepted the Torah because of the thunders and lightnings which occurred at Sinai, while the proselyte who had not witnessed these things nevertheless surrendered himself. Many other quotations could be cited from the Rabbis to support the view that they welcomed proselytes. In an illuminating article on this period Rabbi Sidney Hoenig sums up, 'There is not the slightest shadow of a doubt that the prevailing feeling towards proselytes was very favourable'.

There can also be no doubting the fact that a great deal of proselytization did take place, and at times it must have been fairly intense. In the New Testament Book of Matthew, the Jewish Scribes and Pharisees are described as travelling 'over sea and land to win one convert' (Matthew 23:15). The Anglo-Jewish historian, Cecil Roth, has written that 'within a century from the Hasmonean revolt, the area of the Jewish state was increased perhaps tenfold, and its population in proportion. It is from the ethnic group formed in these years that the Jewish people of today is predominantly descended'. Similarly, the American writer Max I Dimont estimates that in the first century 10 per cent of the Roman Empire was Jewish—seven million out of 70 million. Of these seven million only four million were of Jewish descent, the remainder must have been converts. Far from passively sitting back and accepting proselytes, it is clear that the Jews had been very active in making converts, and it was only Church and State legislation forbidding the conversion of Christians to Judaism which forced Jews back into their shell. As so often happens, as the years passed by, some Jews began to make a virtue out of necessity by declaring that Judaism was not a missionary religion. The fact is that Judaism always has accepted the duty to receive sincere proselytes, and that remains the situation in our own time.

There is a difference, however, in the general approach to would-be proselytes by the Orthodox and the Liberal

Jewish authorities. The Orthodox *Beth Din* usually rejects any application which arises in connection with inter-marriage, following the dictum, 'He who embraces Judaism to marry a Jewess, or through love or fear of Jews, is not a genuine proselyte' (Ger. 1:3). However, a small number of proselytes do finally succeed and, having satisfied the Orthodox requirements with regard to knowledge and practice, are accepted into Judaism after they have been immersed in a ritual bath (*Tevilah*) and, in the case of men, after circumcision has been performed.

Liberal Judaism treats every application for proselytiza-tion on its own merits. The proselyte is first interviewed by a Minister to ascertain the motives for conversion. We too regard the intention to marry a Jew as being inadequate by itself, but not as disqualifying the applicant. We must be satisfied that the applicant is desirous of embracing the Jewish religion for its own sake, and in order to assist the applicant to make an informed decision we insist upon some preliminary reading and experience of Jewish life and wor-ship. Usually the applicant attends synagogue services for at least three months before he (or she) embarks upon a more formal course of instruction. This course consists of lessons in the Jewish religion, Jewish history, Jewish literature and the Hebrew language. During the course, the applicant should gain personal experience of all the Jewish festivals in the yearly cycle, and he should also begin to feel himself as part of a Jewish congregation.

When the instructor is satisfied that a sufficient basis of Jewish knowledge and experience has been acquired, and the applicant has shown a sincere attitude, then an appoint-ment is made for the candidate to be interviewed by a Rabbinic Board of the Rites and Practices Committee of the Union of Liberal and Progressive Synagogues. If the three Rabbis on this Board are satisfied with the sincerity and knowledge of the candidate they sign a certificate indicating that they have approved the application. A ceremony is later conducted in the synagogue where the candidate received instruction, during which the candidate recites a prayer of allegiance to Judaism and to the Jewish people before the open Ark, and the *Shema* is also recited. The Minister usually recites the ancient priestly benediction, gives the proselyte a Hebrew name, and adds his signature (together with the signatures of two witnesses) to the proselyte certificate. We are careful to point out to all proselytes that, while they will be accepted as Jews by every Progressive Jewish congregation throughout the world, nevertheless because of their different rules for the acceptance of proselytes, the Orthodox Jewish authorities will not necessarily accept them. All proselytes sign a form to the effect that this has been pointed out to them.

We urge male candidates to undergo circumcision before their application is submitted to the Rabbinic Board unless some compelling reason is produced for exemption. We do not require immersion in a ritual bath although some Liberal Jewish circles are considering it carefully. Many congregations invite a lady proselyte to kindle the Sabbath candles at the commencement of the evening service on the Sabbath immediately following her admission, and a male proselyte might be invited to open the Ark or be called to the Torah. In this way, public recognition is given to their acceptance into the life of the congregation. The children of a proselyte, under the age of seven, are accepted into Judaism with the admission of their parent. Children between seven and 16 do not receive automatic recognition but are expected to attend Religion School until they reach Confirmation, which then 'seals' their Jewish status. It remains merely to repeat that Liberal Judaism affirms the duty to accept sincere proselytes, and looks forward to the fulfilment of the prophecy of Zechariah: 'It shall come to pass that ten men shall take hold, out of all the languages of the nations, shall even take hold of the skirt of him that is a Jew, saying: We will go with you, for we have heard that God is with you' (Zech. 8:23).

17 And a Time to Die

Rituals relating to death

Judaism is often described as 'a way of life' yet it is strange that so many Jews only make contact with their synagogue when the death of a loved one is imminent or has occurred! Nevertheless, just as there are rituals which welcome a person into life, so there are rituals which bid him adieu. The Liberal Jewish prayerbook contains a number of prayers to be recited by a person who is critically ill, or by someone on his behalf, concluding with the great Jewish declaration of faith—the *Shema*.

Once death has occurred, a number of rituals are performed, and it might be useful to summarize first the Orthodox procedure and then indicate where Liberal Judaism differs. First, the eyes are closed, the body is arranged in a certain way, and a lighted candle is placed near the head. Until the funeral, the body is attended day and night by a 'watcher' (*Wacher* in Yiddish). Before the funeral, the body is washed according to a prescribed ritual called Tohorah (Purification), then wrapped in shrouds (*Tachrichim*) and, in the case of a man, his *Tallit* (Prayer-shawl), before being placed in a plain wooden coffin. Traditionally, all this is done by a Burial Society (*Chevrah Kaddisha*). Based on a Scriptural law, which relates to the body of an executed criminal, Judaism requires that the burial should take place as soon as possible after death.

Orthodox Judaism insists on burial, regarding the alternative of cremation as a pagan custom, disrespectful to the dead and at variance with the belief in physical resurrection.

Nor does Orthodox Judaism permit a *Cohen* (one reputedly descended from the ancient priesthood) to come within a distance of four cubits from a coffin—except at the burial of a close relative—in order not to 'defile' himself by 'contact with the dead'. In some communities, including Anglo-Jewry, it is generally supposed that women should not attend a funeral, but there is no sound basis for this supposition either in Jewish tradition or in psychology. Immediately before the burial, it is customary among Orthodox Jews for the next of kin to make a tear in their garments as a mark of grief. This is called *Keriah* (Rending).

The mourning that takes place after the funeral is called *Avelut*. It consists of three stages of diminishing intensity. The first is called *Shivah* (Seven) and lasts for seven days beginning on the day of the funeral. During this period the next of kin (father, mother, husband, wife, brother, sister, son, daughter) stay at home, sit on low stools and abstain from bathing, cutting their hair, shaving, and wearing leather shoes. Many resort to the superstitious practice of covering mirrors. A service is held in the home daily throughout the period so that the mourner's prayer (*Kaddish*) can be recited, and candles are kept burning throughout the seven days. Friends call in to condole with them and often bring them food. The second stage of mourning is called *Sheloshim* (30) and lasts for 30 days from the day of the funeral. During this period the mourners are supposed to abstain from cutting their hair, wearing freshly pressed clothes and attending joyful festivities. Finally, there is an eleven month period during which, in the case of a parent, the sons have to recite the Mourner's *Kaddish* three times daily and to keep away from joyful festivities. At the end of the period a tombstone (*Matzevah*) is erected over the grave.

Liberal Judaism does not find it easy to lay down precise rules in these matters since mourning is something personal and depends so much upon the temperament and outlook of the individual. If people feel grief, they have little need of externally imposed forms to express it. If they do not feel grief, then the observance of such form would be hypo-critical. As a result of this attitude, Liberal Jewish practice, allowing for individual differences and respecting the individual's freedom of choice, has developed the following general procedure when death occurs.

Liberal Judaism believes that the nurses who have tended the person during the final hours of his life can confidently be entrusted to wash his body at death. Consequently most Liberal synagogues (with one or two exceptions) do not have a Burial Society in the traditional sense. We also recommend that burial takes place without undue delay, although it may occasionally be necessary to allow time for a post-mortem, or to wait for the arrival of a particularly close relative from abroad. We agree that a standard plain coffin should be used in order to make no distinction between rich and poor at death. We see no good reason for differentiating between cremation and burial as legitimate and honourable means of disposal of the body and, therefore, a Liberal Jewish Minister would officiate at a service in a Crematorium. We do not prevent a *Cohen* from coming close to a coffin, nor do we discourage women from attending funerals.

It is customary for a service to be held in the home on the first evening after the funeral, but we do not consider it necessary or even desirable to tear clothes, sit on low stools, cover mirrors, etc. Obviously we do not forbid these customs if the mourners wish to observe them, but if our guidance is sought we would discourage them. It is also left to the mourners to decide whether additional evening services in the home will be helpful during their bereavement; likewise how much 'austerity' they consider is appropriate to practise during the ensuing period of mourning, and for how long. We would advise them to attend services in the synagogue, but of course this does not apply only to mourners!

The name of the deceased is usually mentioned in the synagogue before the recital of the *Kaddish* during the Sabbath service after burial has taken place. Another service, to dedicate the tombstone (*Matzevah*) is usually held at the cemetery about a year after burial. The anniversary (*Yahrzeit* in Yiddish) of a parent's death is observed by lighting a memorial candle in the home. It is also customary to have the deceased's name mentioned in the synagogue before the recital of the *Kaddish* during the Sabbath service nearest to the anniversary. The date of the anniversary may be calculated either according to the Hebrew or the secular calendar. A number of Memorial (*Yizkor*) services are held in the synagogue during the year particularly on *Yom Kippur* afternoon and the last day of *Pesach*. A Memorial service is also held at the Liberal Jewish cemetery on the Sunday before *Rosh Hashanah*.

Judaism tries to teach its adherents an acceptance of death within the general scheme of things. As Sirach advised, 'Do not fear the summons of death; remember those who have gone before you, and those who will come after you. This is the Lord's decree for all flesh' (41:3-4). It also teaches a belief in spiritual immortality. We are urged to praise God at all times, as Job declared: 'The Lord has given, and the Lord has taken away, blessed be the name of the Lord' (Job 1:21) and we are urged to strive for the coming of His kingdom (as emphasized in the *Kaddish*). Finally, we are reminded of the words in Ecclesiastes (3:2): 'To everything there is a season . . . a time to be born and a time to die'. Judaism teaches us to live responsibly and to die serenely, confident in the assurance that the Eternal God is our Guardian in life and death.

References

PART I
Page 1. HOW BEAUTIFUL OUR HERITAGE!

3 **. . . a pamphlet setting out the general principles:**
The Jewish Religious Union: Its Principles and its Future, 2nd
edition 1918. Pub. Jewish Religious Union.

3 **. . . a manifesto outlining its practical programme:**
see Lily H. Montagu, *The Jewish Religious Union and Its
Beginnings*, (pamphlet) 1927. Pub. Jewish Religious Union.

2. THE HERITAGE OF THE CONGREGATION OF JACOB

6 **. . . as the Bible testifies:** see, e.g., the many inter-
marriages mentioned in the Bible and the reference to the
'mixed multitude' in Exodus 12:38.

7 **. . . 'his old ideal of the Englishman of the Jewish
faith':** from a lecture given by Claude G. Montefiore to
the Society for the Study of Religion. See Lucy Cohen,
Some Recollections of Claude Goldsmid Montefiore, pages 227f.

8 **. . . 'people of religion':** See I. I. Mattuck's book, *What
are the Jews? Their Significance and Position in the Modern
World*, 1939. Pub. Hodder & Stoughton.

8 **. . . urged moderation on both sides:** see, e.g., I. I.
Mattuck's important letter in *The Times*, 19 April 1948,
republished in the *Liberal Jewish Monthly*, May 1948.

8 **. . . Less typical was his Associate Rabbi, Maurice
L. Perlzweig:** see the fascinating debate between Monte-
fiore and Maurice Perlzweig published by the Jewish
Religious Union in 1935 as a pamphlet entitled: *Why the
Jewish Religious Union can be, and justifiably is, 'neutral' as
regards Zionism.*

8   **... nothing Jewish alien to me:** This is an adaptation of Terence's *Homo sum; humani nil a me alienum puto.*

3. SING TO THE LORD A NEW SONG

10   **... and the Men of the Great Assembly:** Avot 1:1. Note that the line of succession is a lay, not a priestly one.

12   **... 'sing to the Lord a new song':** Isa. 42:10, Psalms 33:3, 96:1, 98:1, 144:9, 149:1.

4. THE SEAL OF GOD

13   **... such an affirmation:** according to the Shulchan Aruch (Orach Chayyim 124:6), when the worshipper responds 'Amen', he should say to himself: 'True is the benediction which the precentor has recited, and I believe in it.'

13   **... 'Thirteen Principles of the Faith':** see 'Singer's' *Authorised Daily Prayer Book*, current edition, pp. 93-95. Maimonides' original version occurs in his Mishnah Commentary on the 10th chapter of Sanhedrin and runs to over 5,000 words.

13   **... 'the Torah is not from Heaven':** Sanh. 10:1. It is to be noted, however, that this can also be translated, '... that there is no Torah from Heaven', in which case the 'heresy' consists, not in denying that the whole Torah is divinely revealed, but that any of it is.

14   **... 'Only he can be considered':** Solomon Eger, quoted by David Philipson in *The Reform Movement in Judaism*, new edition 1930. Pub. Ktav Publishing Inc.

15   **... Claude Montefiore in a sermon he preached:** C. G. Montefiore, *Truth in Religion and other sermons*, 1906. Pub. Macmillan & Co.

5. THE BEGINNING OF WISDOM

18   **... as 'God-intoxicated':** remark attributed to Novalis (Friedrich von Hardenberg).

20   **... 'there are more things in heaven and earth ...':** William Shakespeare, *Hamlet* I, V, 166.

21   **... Let there be light:** *Gate of Repentance*, p. 182, from a sonnet by Robert Nathan.

6. OUR GOD AND OUR FATHERS' GOD

22   **. . . 'Hear, O Israel':** Deut. 6:4, *Service of the Heart*, p. 32. Montefiore and Mattuck thought not: Montefiore, *Outlines of Liberal Judaism*, Chapter VI, 1912. Pub. Macmillan & Co. Mattuck, *Essentials of Liberal Judaism*, pp. 34-39, 1947. Pub. George Routledge & Sons.

24   **. . . laid great stress:** *Mishneh Torah, Hilchot Y'sodey ha-Torah* 1:9.

26   **. . . 'The Lord, the Lord God is merciful':** Ex. 34:6f; *Gate of Repentance*, p. 76. It is noteworthy that in the traditional Jewish liturgy the word 'acquitting' is retained but the words 'does not acquit' are omitted, so that even the 13th attribute, contrary to the plain meaning of Scripture, is understood as a synonym for God's mercy.

27   **. . . a famous comment on these words:** attributed to Israel ben Eliezer, the Baal Shem Tov.

7. A LITTLE LESS THAN DIVINE

28   **. . . in Jewish folklore:** It is noteworthy, however, that angels are not mentioned in the Mishnah.

31   **. . . 'a compassionate, torn and sorrowing God':** Meyer Levin, *The Fanatic*, p. 28, 1964. Pub. Simon & Schuster, New York.

31   **. . . Judaism has consistently condemned:** see, e.g., Isa. 45:7 and the frequent condemnations in Rabbinic literature of those who assert that there are *sh'tey r'shuyyot*, 'two powers' in control of the universe.

32   **. . . 'the belief in a supernatural source of evil':** Nicholas Bentley & Evan Esar, *The Treasury of Humorous Quotations*, p. 61, 1962. Pub. J. M. Dent & Sons.

32   **. . . 'To us there is but one atonement':** Montefiore, *Outlines of Liberal Judaism*, p. 306, 1912. Pub. Macmillan & Co.

8. THE END OF DAYS

34   **. . . 'revive the dead':** see, e.g., 'Singer's' *Authorised Daily Prayer Book*, current edition, pp. 46f; *Liberal Jewish Prayer Book*, Vol. I 1937 edition, Introduction, page XV; *Service of the Heart*, p. 45 and Note 60, p. 472.

35   **. . . our current liturgy:** see, e.g., *Service of the Heart,* pp. 84, 141 and Note 195, p. 486; *Gate of Repentance,* pp. 42, 112, 370, 372.

37   **. . . 'On account of our sins':** 'Singer's' *Authorised Daily Prayer Book,* current edition, pp. 319f.

9. A LIGHT TO THE NATIONS

39   **. . . 'We will do and obey':** Mechilta to Ex. 20:22, quoting Ex. 24:7.

41   **. . . 'A kingdom of priests':** Morris Joseph, *Judaism as Creed and Life,* 5th edition, 1925, pp. 159f. Pub. George Routledge & Sons (republished Reform Synagogues of Great Britain).

41   **. . . 'the Pharisees and Rabbis':** Bernard J. Bamberger, *Proselytism in the Talmudic Period,* p. 274, 1939. Pub. Hebrew Union College Press, Cincinnatti.

42   **. . . the acceptance of converts:** See, for instance, the fascinating exchange between Mattuck and Montefiore published by the Jewish Religious Union in 1933 in a pamphlet entitled *Jewish Views on Jewish Missions;* also Mattuck's clear analysis of the problem, 'The Missionary Idea', in the volume, *Aspects of Progressive Jewish Thought,* edited by him, 1954. Pub. Victor Gollancz.

42   **. . . 'the homing impulse in Judaism':** David Polish, *The Eternal Dissent* p. 148, no date. Pub. Abbelard-Schuman Ltd.

10. THE WORD OF THE LORD

45   **. . . such as Adam and Noah:** These so-called Noachide Laws are generally said to number seven and to include the prohibitions against idolatry, incest, murder, blasphemy, robbery and vivisection as well as the injunction to establish law-courts.

45   **. . . that is to say, the Patriarchs:** for instance, Abraham was commanded concerning circumcision; see Gen. 17:9-14.

45   **. . . God proclaimed the Ten Commandments.** Sometimes the Rabbis say that only the first two Commandments were so proclaimed by God Himself, the rest mediated by Moses; see, e.g., Makkot 24a.

46   **... be called 'Torah':** The word Torah means 'teaching', but in the specific sense of a teaching believed to emanate from God. At first it referred to an individual teaching of this kind, so that it could be used in the plural; see, e.g., Ex. 18:16. Then it came to be used collectively, for the entire body of divine teachings. Since these teachings concern, in the main, God's will rather than His nature, they are generally couched in the imperative or jussive; hence the common translation of Torah as 'Law'. The Prophets often refer to their own teachings as Torah; see, e.g., Isa. 1:10. The words of Psalm 78:1, 'Give ear, O my people, to my Torah', gave rise to the comment that 'the Prophets and Hagiographa are also Torah'; see, e.g., Solomon Schechter, *Aspects of Rabbinic Theology*, pp. 122f, 1961. Pub. Schocken (paperback), first published 1909.

49   **... Thus, to quote Louis Jacobs:** Louis Jacobs, *A Jewish Theology*, p. 213, 1973. Pub. Darton Longman & Todd.

49   **... 'Error as well as truth':** *Ibid.*, p. 209.

50   **... 'Did God really say ...?:** Gen. 3:1; see, e.g., Louis Jacobs, *Jewish Values*, p. 25, 1960. Pub. Vallentine, Mitchell.

Page 11. WHAT DOES THE LORD YOUR GOD REQUIRE OF YOU?

53   **... 'the study of Torah is equal to them all':** Peah 1:1; compare with *Service of the Heart*, p. 248.

55   **... 'stubborn and rebellious son'.:** Deut. 21:18-21; B.B. 126b, Sanh. 68b-71a.

12. THESE ARE THE THINGS WHICH YOU SHALL DO

62   **... women in traditional Judaism:** For a general discussion of this topic see John D. Rayner, *Guide to Jewish Marriage*, 1975. Pub. U.L.P.S., especially chapter 3, and his essay, 'Women's Status in Judaism' in *Reform Judaism*, ed. by Rabbi Dow Marmur, 1973. Pub. R.S.G.B.

65   **... teachings of the Prophets:** For an excellent summary of the essential teachings of the Prophets, see I. I. Mattuck, *The Thought of the Prophets*, 1953. Pub. George Allen & Unwin.

13. THAT YOU MAY REMEMBER

69   ... **can hardly be exaggerated:** For some further thoughts on prayer, see *Service of the Heart*, pp. 3-12.

70   ... **'the value of Jewish ceremonies':** I. I. Mattuck, *The Essentials of Liberal Judaism*, p. 152, 1947. Pub. George Routledge & Sons.

70   ... **Elsewhere he added:** (pamphlet) I. I. Mattuck, *Liberal Judaism: Its thought and practice*, pp. 16f, 1947. Pub. U.L.P.S.

PART II

Page   1. TO LIFE

76   ... **as Dr. Hertz commented:** *Commentary on Exodus*, p. 223, 1935. Pub. Oxford University Press.

76   ... **In the Midrash we find:** Sifra on Lev. 25:36.

2. LOVE YOUR NEIGHBOUR

79   ... **not to kill:** Ex. 20:13
not to kidnap: Ex. 20:13
not to rob: Lev. 19:13
not to steal: Lev. 19:11
not to oppress: Lev. 19:13
not to deceive: Lev. 19:11
not to defraud: Lev. 25:14
not to humiliate: Lev. 25:17
not to swear falsely: Ex. 20:7
not to testify falsely: Ex. 20:13
not to ignore lost property: Deut. 22:3
not to lead astray: Lev. 19:14
not to gossip: Lev. 19:16
not to hate: Lev. 19:17
not to take vengeance: Lev. 19:18
not to bear any grudge: Lev. 19:18
not to covet: Deut. 5:18
to imitate God: Deut. 28:9
to give to the poor: Det. 15:11; Lev. 25:35ff.
to pay wages promptly: Deut. 24:15
to love strangers: Deut. 10:19
to honour one's parents: Ex. 20:12
to act correctly in business: Ex. 22:13; Lev. 25:14

81 ... **Maimonides summed up:** Mishneh Torah, Hilchot Matt'not Aniyyim, ch. 10

3. A LITTLE SANCTUARY

83 ... **a 'little sanctuary':** Ezek. 11:16.

85 ... **'Proper education in contraception':** Rabbinical Assembly.

85 ... **'We urge the recognition':** Central Conference of American Rabbis.

6. YOU SHALL NOT DESTROY

99 ... **the late Albert Schweitzer:** q.Arvill: *Man and Environment*, p. 315.

99 ... **Robert Arvill** in his *Man and Environment*, p. 316. Pub. Penguin Books.

103 ... **Jewish historian, Josephus:** *Antiquities of the Jews*, XV. 7:1.

7. TO LEARN AND TO TEACH

106 ... **Jewish daughters did not have to be taught:** Mishnah Sot. 3:4; Kid. 29b.

108 ... **According to Jewish law:** Meg. 27a.

110 ... **As Mordechai Kaplan put it:** *Future of the American Jew*, p. 44.

Page 8. SERVICE OF THE HEART

112 ... **four passages from the Pentateuch:** Ex. 13:1-10. Ex. 13:11-16. Deut. 6:4-9. Deut. 11:13-21.

113 ... **Emil G. Hirsch wrote:** *Reform Advocate*, 1892, iii. 109.

10. OBSERVE THE SABBATH DAY

123 ... **the context of the act of Creation:** Gen. 2:3, Ex. 31:16-17.

123 ... **one of the Ten Commandments:** Ex. 20:8, Deut. 5:12.

11. DAYS OF AWE

130 ... **all U.L.P.S. congregations except one:** Belsize Square Synagogue.

. . . That is why we make the gesture of 'fasting': Traditionally, the custom of fasting is derived from the Biblical designation of the Day of Atonement as a day of 'self-affliction' (Lev. 16:29, 23:27).

12. THREE TIMES IN THE YEAR

136 **. . . a repeated prohibition in the Pentateuch:** Ex. 12 and 13, *passim.*
Chag ha-Shavuot: Ex. 34:22. Deut. 16:9.
Shavuot: Num. 28:26.

13. JOY AND GLADNESS

142 **. . . lacking in religious motivation:** see, e.g., Rabbi John Rayner's article in the *Liberal Jewish Monthly*, March 1962.

143 **. . . One Liberal Jewish Congregation:** Finchley Progressive Synagogue.

14. ALL YOUR CHILDREN SHALL BE TAUGHT OF THE LORD

146 **. . . Liberal Jews observe the practice:** Rayner, *Liberal Judaism*, (pamphlet) p. 15.

15. THE VOICE OF THE BRIDEGROOM AND THE VOICE OF THE BRIDE

151 **. . . only the child of a Jewish mother is Jewish:** Mishnah Kid. 3:12.

154 **. . . the pig and the hare:** Lev. 11:2-8, Deut. 14:4-8.

154 **. . . lobsters and the like:** Lev. 11:9-12, Deut. 14:11-18.

155 **. . . specifically permits may be eaten:** Lev. 11:13-19, Deut. 14:11-18.

155 **. . . exception of locusts:** Lev. 11:20-23, 29-30, 41-42; Deut. 14:19-20.

155 **. . . died of itself:** Deut. 14:21.

155 **. . . it is injured:** Ex. 22:30.

155 **. . . blood was considered forbidden:** Lev. 3:13, 7:26, 17:12-14.

155 **. . . forbids certain fats:** Lev. 7:23.

155 **. . . sinew that shrank:** Gen. 32:33.

155   ... **boil a kid in its mother's milk:** Ex. 23:19, 34:26, Deut. 14:21.

Page   16. YOUR GOD SHALL BE MY GOD

158   ... **Dr. Claude Montefiore has pointed out:** Montefiore and Loewe, *A Rabbinic Anthology*, p. 566, 1960. Pub. Jewish Publication Society of America.

158   ... **for the native and for the ger:** Ex. 12:49, Lev. 24:22, Num. 9:14, 15:15, 16, 29, Deut. 1:16.

158   ... **love him as yourself:** Lev. 19:34.

158   ... **Rabbi Albert Goldstein has pointed out:** *Conversion to Judaism*, ed. Max Eichhorn, p. 26. Pub. Ktav Publishing House Inc.

159   ... **Rabbi Bernard Bamberger put it:** Ibid. pp. 179-180.

160   ... **Israelites who stood around Mt. Sinai:** Mid. Tan. Lech Lecha 6, ed. Buber, 32.

160   ... **Rabbi Sidney Hoenig sums up:** *Conversion to Judaism*, p. 56 (See above).

160   ... **Cecil Roth, has written:** *A Short History of the Jewish People*, p. 79, 1936. Macmillan & Co.

160   **Max I. Dimont estimates:** *Jews, God and History*, p. 113. Pub. The New American Library Inc.

17. AND A TIME TO DIE

163   ... **a person who is critically ill:** *Service of the Heart*, p. 436 and pp. 440-441.

NOTE

Service of the Heart and *Gate of Repentance*, which are both mentioned repeatedly in the text of this book, are respectively the prayerbooks for the weekday, Sabbath and Festival services and prayers for home and synagogue, and services for the High Holydays of the Union of Liberal and Progressive Synagogues. They were both edited jointly by Rabbi John D. Rayner and Rabbi Chaim Stern and were published respectively in 1967 and 1973 by the U.L.P.S.

U.L.P.S. PUBLICATIONS

SERVICE OF THE HEART

The prayerbook for Sabbath, Festivals and weekdays
includes sections for the consecration of events such as
marriage, the birth of a child and moving into a new home.
Its prayers, meditations and themes on justice, brotherhood,
etc., reflect the religious concerns through the life cycle of
the Jew. All Hebrew passages are translated into English.
Edited by John D. Rayner and Chaim Stern.

GATE OF REPENTANCE

The prayerbook for the Jewish New Year and Day of
Atonement contains a wealth of liturgical creativity, both
ancient and modern. Its prayers, meditations and narratives
mirror the religious anxieties and aspirations of the Jewish
soul on the holiest days of the Jewish Year. All Hebrew
passages are translated into English.
Edited by John D. Rayner and Chaim Stern.

GUIDE TO JEWISH MARRIAGE
by John D. Rayner

This is a resource work on Jewish marriage customs and laws
which gives the historical background to Jewish attitudes and
considers the difference between Orthodox and Progressive
Judaism on this sensitive subject.

These books are published by the Union of Liberal and
Progressive Synagogues. Further literature on Progressive
Judaism or information regarding U.L.P.S. synagogues may
be obtained from the Union of Liberal and Progressive
Synagogues, The Montagu Centre, 109 Whitfield Street,
London, WIP 5RP.